William
Booth

WOMEN OF FAITH SERIES

Amy Carmichael
Catherine Marshall
Corrie ten Boom
Fanny Crosby
Florence Nightingale
Gladys Aylward

Harriet Tubman
Isobel Kuhn
Joni Eareckson Tada
Madame Guyon
Mary Slessor
Susanna Wesley

MEN OF FAITH SERIES

Andrew Murray
Borden of Yale
Brother Andrew
C. S. Lewis
Charles Colson
Charles Finney
Charles Spurgeon
D. L. Moody
David Brainerd
E. M. Bounds
Eric Liddell
George Müller
Hudson Taylor
Jim Elliot

John Calvin
John Hyde
John Newton
John Paton
John Wesley
Jonathan Edwards
Jonathan Goforth
Luis Palau
Martin Luther
Oswald Chambers
Samuel Morris
William Booth
William Carey

WOMEN AND MEN OF FAITH

John and Betty Stam
Francis and Edith Schaeffer

OTHER BIOGRAPHIES FROM BETHANY HOUSE

Autobiography of Charles Finney (Wessel)
Behind the Stories (Eble)
Janette Oke: A Heart for the Prairie (Logan)
Miracle in the Mirror (Buntain)
Of Whom the World Was Not Worthy (Jakob Kovac family)
Out of Mormonism (Robertson)
Success by Design (Hirsch)
Where Does a Mother Go to Resign (Johnson)

William Booth

David Bennett

BETHANY HOUSE PUBLISHERS
MINNEAPOLIS, MINNESOTA 55438

William Booth
Copyright © 1986
David Bennett

Cover by Dan Thornberg

Library of Congress Catalog Card Number 93–74544

ISBN 1–55661–307–5

Originally published in English by Marshall, Morgan &
Scott Publications Ltd. (now part of HarperCollins
Publishers, Ltd.) under the title
William Booth and the Salvation Army,
© 1986 (David Bennett).

Published by Bethany House Publishers
A Ministry of Bethany Fellowship International
11400 Hampshire Avenue South
Minneapolis, Minnesota 55438
www.bethanyhouse.com

Printed in the United States of America by
Bethany Press International
Minneapolis, Minnesota 55438

Dedication

To my mother and father,
who know what it is
to have been poor.

Acknowledgements

The following members of The Salvation Army supplied helpful information for the writing of this book: Ray Allen, Cyril Barnes, George Ellis, and Jenty Fairbank. I extend my warm appreciation to them.

Preface

This is the true story of William Booth and the early soldiers of the Salvation Army. Though all of the incidents in this book actually happened, on occasions the sequence or nature of events has been slightly altered.

The real names of a few of the characters, who play minor roles in our story, have been lost in the passage of time. I have taken the liberty of renaming them. Though some of the dialogue is imagined, much of it is as recorded by the participants.

David Bennett

Contents

PART THREE: THE WORLD

1

A Walk in the Night

The preacher, tall and erect, walked swiftly westward along London's Mile End Road. He wore a high hat and neat, though cheap, clothes. His black beard was flecked with gray, dishevelled but clean. His piercing eyes scanned the miserable sights that he passed. The East End of London today is scarcely the world's most prosperous area, but in 1865 it was a place of utmost poverty and moral degradation.

Around him were the people who were to become his life's work. Though it was well after 10 P.M., children—dirty, slovenly and uncared for—scurried at his feet. Their fathers and mothers were in the gin palaces spending what little money they had, and fighting in drunken anger. Other women were left in their hovels, which masqueraded as homes, feeding the latest additions to already over-large families, or working for a pittance at stitchwork and making cane baskets, clothes pegs, and matchboxes.

Filth, noise, and stench pervaded the whole area. The filth of uncleared garbage, the noise of screaming hags, shouting men and playing children and the stench of streets with hardly a semblance of sanitation. Street salesmen peddled their wares to anyone fortunate enough to be able to buy them. These dim, gas-lit streets were the home of every imaginable form of vice and human suffering.

The tall man had been preaching on the Mile End Waste to a mocking crowd amused by the novelty of an open-air preacher in their territory. Bible in hand, he had proclaimed Jesus Christ to an accompaniment of jeers, catcalls, and derision. His Nottinghamshire accent had not helped him reach his cockney listeners.

William Booth's long steps took him quickly past the pubs, dance halls, and other places of amusement. He had to hurry, for his home in Hammersmith was over eight miles away, and his wife Catherine would be concerned at his late arrival. She was two months pregnant with their seventh child. The children—from William (Willie), aged nine years, to Marian, just over a year—slept, but not all slept soundly. All of the Booth children were to grow to adulthood but, as was common with large Victorian families, sickness seemed a constant companion. Marian was subject to fits from an early age.

He walked on, more and more saddened by the sights that met his eyes, his sensitive nature and love for humanity touched by the moral pollution that he witnessed all around. *Where can you find such heathen as these?* he thought. No need to go overseas. No need to tour England, visiting Cornwall, Yorkshire, and any other county that called upon his evangelistic endeavors. These Londoners needed him. More importantly they needed Christ, and very few outsiders, it seemed to Booth, cared.

John Pounds, founder of the Ragged School Union, had been working in that area for more than twenty years, and Pounds was not alone. There were others who cared, but none were to show it as well or make the impact that Booth was to make in the years ahead. This surely must be his life's work—to preach the Gospel to these despairing people. His sense of duty overcame his natural fear, for he knew that death lurked on every corner in the notorious East End. The reformer Edwin Chadwick had estimated that over 10,000 people met violent death annually in Britain, mostly in such slum areas as he was journeying through.

Booth passed through the East London streets, on to the city, and approached more prosperous areas. As he walked along the Strand, which Disraeli called the "first street in Europe," a prostitute emerged from a doorway. She was garishly dressed and her purpose was obvious.

"How about it, Mister?" she offered.

"Give up your evil way and turn to Christ," replied the

preacher. He fumbled in his pocket and pulled out a tract, which he handed to her. "Read that. Read that," he urged, and continued on his way.

The woman looked down at the piece of paper in her hand. It meant nothing to her, because she was illiterate, so she crumpled it up and threw it down in contempt.

She glanced at an old woman, her guardian, who had been keeping a very close eye on the exchange, and said, "Trust me to pick a bloomin' choker. Trust me!"

The old woman cackled gleefully, but said nothing.

He walked on through the wealthy West End, and on to his modest home in Hammersmith. It was after midnight when he arrived, but Catherine was still up, having preached to the "upper classes" herself that evening. To high society a woman preacher was as great a novelty as a man with two heads.

Booth wasn't his usual affectionate self this night. His mind was in too much of a turmoil, and he threw his hat almost despairingly onto a table and flung himself into an armchair.

"Oh, Kate!" he blurted out. "As I passed by the doors of those gin palaces tonight, I seemed to hear a voice saying, 'Where can you find such heathen as these, and where is there so great a need for your labours?' I felt as though I ought at all costs to stop and preach to those East End multitudes."

Catherine gazed into the fire. Into her mind came doubts. *This means another new venture, another start in life,* she thought. "How can we make enough to support our family among the poverty-stricken East-Enders? Up to now we have had the financial support of my more 'respectable' audiences, but if we throw in our lot with the poor that income will disappear."

She checked her anxieties in a moment of silent prayer, and turned to her husband. "Well, if you feel we ought to do this, we shall do it. We have trusted the Lord once for our support and we can trust Him again," she said boldly.

That night, in spirit if not in name, the Salvation Army was born.

2

Early Days

Catherine Booth was born Catherine Mumford at Ashbourne in Derbyshire on January 17, 1829. A bright, intelligent child, she could read at the age of three after the minimum of instruction, and by the time she was twelve had read the Bible right through from Genesis to Revelation eight times.

Her parents, John and Sarah, were faithful Methodists. Catherine was very close to her father, but more distant from her rather austere mother.

She did not go to school until she was twelve and was basically reserved and shy, but when roused her intense, passionate nature overcame her timidity. At the age of nine she witnessed a policeman dragging along a drunk, followed by a crowd, jeering and tormenting him. Even as a child she hated alcoholic drink, but she also detested unkindness and was immediately filled with pity for the man. She ran to his side, took hold of his hand and, giving the crowd a defiant glare, walked with him and the constable to the police station.

Her lack of schooling did little to impair her education, as she was an ardent reader. But she experienced little of friendships with other children, and had no confidante of her own age. Her main companion was a dog called Waterford. He followed her everywhere.

On one occasion the faithful retriever followed his mistress when she visited her father's business on an errand. She entered the building, leaving him outside. As she walked through the office, she stubbed her toe and cried out in pain. The dog, hearing her cry, rushed to her side, crashing through a large window in the process.

As Catherine, now more concerned about her pet than her foot, checked the animal for injury, a furious John Mumford appeared on the scene. Surveying the damage angrily, he ordered the dog to be shot, in spite of the impassioned pleas of his only daughter.

She was eventually sent to a girls' school in Boston, Lincolnshire where her family was living, not just to improve her education but also as a cure for her increasing tendency to withdraw into herself.

Her time at school was short-lived, as she developed a severe case of curvature of the spine, and at fourteen was forced to spend her time confined to bed, lying face downward. To escape from the pain and boredom she resorted to books, mostly reading church history and theology.

In 1844, when her health had shown a significant improvement, the family moved to Brixton in London.

Two years later Catherine underwent an extreme spiritual struggle. She knew Christian doctrine better than most adults, but she did not know whether she was a Christian or not, and it seemed unreasonable to her to be saved and not know it. She turned to fervent prayer and intense study of the Bible. Often she would pray into the early hours of the morning, walking to and fro in her room in her spiritual anguish.

Before settling down to sleep her normal practice was to place her Bible and hymnbook beneath her pillow. One morning, upon waking she felt under her pillow and pulled out her hymnbook. Opening it at random her eyes alighted upon these lines:

My God, I am Thine,
What a comfort divine,
What a blessing to know that Jesus is mine!

She had often read or sung those words before, but now they suddenly had new meaning. She knew that the words, "My," "I," and "mine" applied to her. "I no longer hoped I was saved," she said, "I was certain of it." She rushed to tell her mother the good news.

William Booth's early days had marked differences from those of his wife-to-be. He was born in the same year, in April, to Samuel and Mary Booth of Nottingham. Mary's name was Moss, and this, along with her decidedly Hebraic features, suggested that she was either partly or totally Jewish. William Booth—and this was especially noticeable in his later years—had distinctly Jewish facial characteristics, as had some of his children.

The Booth family was rather poor and William had to leave school at thirteen to become apprenticed to a pawnbroker. He had no great love for that occupation, and was later to come to detest it, but it taught him much about people, especially the poor, and so it helped equip him for his life's work.

On September 23, 1843, Samuel Booth died. His death made William begin thinking seriously about God, and he joined the local Wesleyan Chapel. Unlike Catherine, his upbringing had been almost totally devoid of religion, but now he became very concerned about his soul's well-being.

He became a Christian in the privacy of his own room, quietly and undramatically. This scarcely anticipated the remarkable conversions which were to come through his future ministry, stretching over more than sixty years.

William Booth was never one to be halfhearted about anything, and he began to throw all his energies into working out his newfound faith. Open-air preaching became his main sphere of activity, but it was not long before he found himself in trouble at his church. Through his open-air work he rounded up a group of tough characters from the Nottingham slums and led them to church, sitting them in the front pews. The sight, smell, and sound of these visitors did not please the congregation, and Booth was warned that if he wanted to continue with this sort of thing his newfound friends would have to sit at the rear of the chapel.

His apprenticeship ended in 1848, and he was unemployed for a year before going to London in the autumn of 1849 to find work. He got a job with a miserly pawnbroker in the London borough of Walworth and attached himself to the Walworth Methodist Chapel. He worked for six days a week with very little spare time in the evenings, and on Sundays usually preached twice at different churches. On occasion he had to run home from church to beat his employer's 10 P.M. curfew.

In 1851 William met a wealthy boot manufacturer, Edward Rabbits, who was to affect his life in two major ways. Rabbits had heard Booth preach and realized how gifted he was. He urged the young evangelist to leave his pawnbroking and take to preaching full-time. On Booth's protesting that he would then have no source of income, Rabbits agreed to support him for three months at £1 a week. So in 1852 William committed his talents to full-time Christian service.

Edward Rabbits also knew the Mumford family. Catherine Mumford had heard William preach and had been greatly impressed, but had never met him. Rabbits unintentionally became their cupid. He held a party at his home, and among the guests invited were the Mumfords and William.

Booth arrived a little late, and Rabbits mischievously tried to make him recite a temperance poem called *The Grog-Seller's Dream* to the audience of abstainers and mild imbibers. Rabbits was very persuasive, and eventually the preacher stood before the gathering and recited the poem, which began:

A grog-seller sat by his bar-room fire,
His feet as high as his head and higher,
Watching the smoke as he puffed it out,
Which in spiral columns curved about . . .

On he read, feeling more and more uncomfortable. The poem was long and told of the publican's encounter with the devil in a dream. Finally he finished and sat down, and a long, embarrassed silence followed.

After what seemed an age a man spoke up and defended his drinking habit. Then a slim young lady with short, curly hair and hands held tightly in her lap proceeded to demolish the man's arguments with sound reasoning, and put forward the case for total abstinence. As others spoke against her views, Catherine Mumford gently but surely answered them with undeniable logic.

William Booth said nothing. He listened and watched Catherine Mumford. That evening the first signs of love stirred in their hearts.

They became engaged in May of that year, but were not married until three years later. In between the engagement and the wedding, Booth entered theological college to study for the ministry of the Methodist New Connexion. He studied under the Rev. Dr. William Cooke, a noted dissenting academic of the Victorian era.

When ordained, William began service in a circuit, a group of churches in one area. It was not long before church leaders noticed his extraordinary evangelistic gifts. Conversions through his ministry were frequent. Many of them were dramatic. He became popular, but also the object of jealousy. Tensions rose about his role in the denomination. Booth became sure that God wanted him to be a full-time evangelist rather than a circuit minister—preaching, pastoring, presiding at meetings, and serving in many different ways.

The matter came to a head at the conference of the Methodist New Connexion of 1861. The debate about his future was one of the main items on the agenda, indicating his standing in the church. The discussion became quite heated, as those who favored Booth's being set aside for a specifically evangelistic task argued with those who opposed the move.

Finally Dr. Cooke proposed a compromise—that Booth should stay in circuit work but be allowed a certain amount of time off to conduct evangelistic crusades. William might have been persuaded, but Catherine was not. She wanted him to be free to pursue his evangelistic ministry unhindered. As Cooke made his proposal, a woman's voice sounded from the gallery and echoed around the church where the conference was held—"No, never!" The assembly looked up, and saw Catherine Booth alone and determined. To her, compromise was unthinkable.

The conference declined to appoint Booth as an evangelist, and eight weeks later he resigned from the Methodist Church. He then became an independent, itinerant evangelist, conducting campaigns throughout Britain and supported by voluntary donations and the income of his wife from her well-to-do audiences.

They had eight children, from William junior (later to be known by his second name, Bramwell) in 1856 to Lucy in 1868.

3

Monk the Prize-Fighter

Peter Monk remembered July 26, 1865, well. It was the day he met a man who was to have a profound influence on his life. Monk was big and tough, an Irish prize-fighter.

He was strolling along, hands in his pockets, on his way to the Blind Beggar public house, when he met a minister of religion, a man as tall as Monk, but made taller by his top hat. Monk was not in the habit of speaking to parsons—indeed, it was a long time since he had met one—but this man had something special about him. Nearly half a century later Monk was to recall, "It was the man's external appearance that attracted me. He was the finest-looking gentleman ever you saw—white-faced, dark-eyed, and a great black beard that fell over his chest. Sure, there was something strange about him that laid hold on a man."

The eyes of Monk and Booth met.

"I'm looking for work," the minister said.

The big-hearted fighter, surprised by this, dived into his pocket to offer him some money, completely misunderstanding the preacher's meaning. But Booth's eyes turned to a group of men outside the public house and extended his hand in their direction. "Look at those men. Look at them! Forgotten by God and man. Where should I be looking for work? There's my work looking for me."

"You're right, sir. Those men are forgotten, and if you can do anything for them it would be a great work," said Monk, taking himself by surprise.

"I'll be preaching on the Mile End Waste in the big tent tomorrow night at seven. Come, and bring these men with you," challenged Booth.

"We'll be there, sir. We'll be there," answered the boxer, his mind scarcely comprehending his own words.

The new day dawned. It was not to be an ordinary day for Peter Monk, for he was due to fight another Irishman called Fitzgerald that afternoon. Fitzgerald was a giant of a man, with as big a reputation, and Monk's mind was in a whirl. He had decided that this would be his last fight. Why? He did not know himself, but he connected it in some strange way with his meeting with the man of God.

The afternoon arrived. The time of the fight was imminent. Monk versus Fitzgerald. Monk was big, but Fitzgerald was larger and as fierce as they came.

In that same year John Chambers had drawn up twelve rules for boxing, including three-minute rounds, a ten-second count after a knockdown, and the wearing of padded gloves. It was to be a long time before these rules were widely accepted, and on this occasion the two fighters were totally unaware of their existence. Boxing in any age is a dangerous sport, but in 1865, with bare fists and a fight to the finish, it was very risky.

Behind the Blind Beggar a crude ring had been set up and a noisy, excited crowd had gathered. The poor of the East End were busily placing their bets on the outcome of the contest.

The fight began. Fitzgerald, not waiting for the customary sizing up of an opponent, made an immediate lunge at Monk, and his bare knuckles slammed into the smaller man's face. The punch momentarily halted Monk in his tracks, but he recovered sufficiently to avoid a swinging right aimed at his head. Monk went in with a left and a right to the body, followed by a right which just missed his opponent's head. Fitzgerald, taking advantage of the other man's loss of balance, threw him hard to the ground, and landed on top of him. That concluded the first round.

As the next round began Monk, still a little shaky on his feet, defended himself against a barrage of blows, but recovered enough to move in and grab hold of Fitzgerald to try to grapple him to the ground. The crowd jostled and swayed in an attempt to get a better view of the two boxers, to the accompaniment of a chorus of cheers and shouts of encouragement.

"Kill 'im, Fitz! Kill 'im!"

"Let's see some blood, Fitzey!" The call rose to a scream in its blind enthusiasm.

"Come on, Monk, get on wiv it! Me muvver could fight better than that."

"'It 'im, Monk! 'It 'im! Don't just stand there."

Monk continued to fight back gamely, giving his opponent a series of stinging blows to the body, which forced Fitzgerald back. A right to the side of the head and a left to the jaw had the bigger man quivering at the knees. Now it was his turn to cover up, only to be pursued by Monk, arms swinging in punch after punch, most of which landed on the defender's protective arms.

The crowd was in a frenzy, pushing and bumping, yelling in support of their particular hero. The fighters responded to the crowd and battled it out. First one then the other would have the advantage. Fitzgerald's left eye became completely closed. Blood poured from Monk's mouth and nose, congealing on his hairy chest.

The crowd became more subdued; the combatants more weary. The blows landed less often, but hurt more. They contented themselves with trying to wrestle each other to the ground. Both secretly wished it would end, but pride made them fight on.

Suddenly Monk found enough energy to unleash a series of pummelling blows to the body with his bloodied hands, and followed it with a stunning punch square on Fitzgerald's jaw. His foe fell in a crumpled heap. It was not the first time that he had been down, but this time he would not get up. After an hour and three-quarters of terrible conflict, Peter Monk, to his own amazement, emerged the victor. "Fitzgerald gave up like an old woman," he recalled years later.

The crowd, cheering and booing, were noisier than before. Monk's supporters grabbed their winnings in great excitement. The loser's fans quickly dispersed with hardly a thought for their fallen hero.

The noise died down. The spectators made their way home. Monk, in his confusion, almost forgot to collect his purse. His thoughts were full of the preacher's invitation. Wearily, he made his way to the tent on the Mile End Waste, entered and stood at the back. The meeting had just begun.

Booth was preaching to a motley gathering of men and women who were jeering, swearing, and hurling insults at the minister. To combat the opposition the evangelist changed his tactics and announced a hymn, which was sung with great gusto by his small band of helpers. Pandemonium broke out, rivalling the noise at the prize-fight—singing, shouting, screaming—it was deafening.

As the hymn drew to an almost unheard conclusion, the boxer made a move. He walked to the front of the crowd, mounted the platform and without saying a word took off his coat and folded his arms across his broad chest. The crowd, most of whom were aware of the fighter's earlier exploit, quieted dramatically.

Booth, a sharp opportunist, took advantage of the silence and launched forth with a Gospel message. His voice was the only one to be heard for the remainder of the meeting.

"How did you do it?" asked Booth at the conclusion of the service. "What happened to your face?"

"I'm a prize-fighter, sir, and I 'ad a fight this afternoon. People in these parts tend to respect a fighter, 'specially a winner, 'specially an Irishman," explained Monk with a grin, which displayed the numerous gaps in his teeth.

"I'm William Booth. What's your name?"

"Monk, sir. Peter Monk."

"You're not happy, Peter Monk. You know you are not happy," challenged the evangelist.

"What reason is that?" questioned Monk, startled.

"You'll perish like a dog. You're living for the devil and the devil will have you."

"Who made a prophet of you?" queried the fighter defensively.

"My Father in heaven," replied Booth.

At that the Irishman looked down at the ground, disturbed. Booth put a hand upon his shoulder and said, "I'll make a man of you yet."

A few days later Monk was kneeling in repentance, tears cascading down his cheeks, aware of his own sinfulness. Challenged by Booth's Christ-given goodness, he got up from the penitent bench a new man.

By the end of that week he was the manager of the East London Mission's soup kitchen. William Booth did not believe in wasting time.

4

Sabotage

*T*he meeting was in full swing, the tent was packed. Booth was leading from the small platform. Half the congregation were seated at the front on rough wooden benches, while the remainder stood at the back. A hymn was being sung with considerable vigor.

Outside a strong wind was blowing and the tent was flapping, adding to the hubbub. Suddenly disaster struck. The tent came loose from its pegs at one end and veered to one side, falling on part of the audience. Chaos broke out as people buried by the tent screamed in panic. Others, with nothing but the sky above them, laughed at the antics of those trying to free themselves.

Booth, determined man though he was, knew that the meeting could not continue. His helpers peeled back the canvas, and gradually the people, recovering from the mishap, left for home or to seek other entertainment.

Peter Monk led a small group to see if the tent could be salvaged. As he stood back and examined the damage, an urgent voice shouted: "Peter! Peter! Look at this!"

Monk hurried over to the man. "What's wrong? What is it?" he asked. James Flawn stood holding a piece of rope in each hand.

"They've been cut, Peter. Cut! Look at 'em! The wind didn't do this, they were cut. I'll tell Mr Booth."

But Monk grabbed Flawn by the shoulders and jolted him round. "No," said the boxer, "he thinks the wind did it. Let him continue to think the wind did it. He has sorrows enough. There is no need to add to them."

The man stood for a moment thoughtfully, held in Monk's

23

powerful grip. "Yes, Peter, you're right. We won't tell him."

The next night Booth, his wife, Monk, Flawn, and a few other mission workers met to discuss the future. The debate centered around the damaged tent. Could it be repaired? If so, at what cost? What was to stop the same thing from happening again? What alternatives were there?

Catherine Booth sat pensively in a chair considering the arguments. Suddenly the answer came to her. "We could hire the dancing saloon in Whitechapel! It's not used on Sundays." She had hardly said a word all evening, and this was a bombshell.

Booth turned toward his wife, his mouth opened to speak, then closed again. He had lived with Catherine long enough to know that her view on anything was not to be taken lightly. Recovering himself, he responded, "But we can't do the Lord's work in a dance hall, my darling."

"Why not?" his wife challenged.

Booth hesitated. "It's not suitable . . . It's just not right."

"Souls can be saved in a dancing hall as well as in a tent or church. And the people are used to going there, so it won't seem strange to them," was Catherine's logical reply.

"Your missis is right, guv," interjected James Flawn. "What difference does it make where we preach, s'long as we preach. And the ropes of a dance hall can't break, can they?"

The meeting erupted in laughter, not least from William Booth.

"They always finish at about two, Sunday mornings, so we can set up the 'all then with our seats and fings," added Flawn.

Booth sat back, stretched his long legs and reflected on the matter, running his bony fingers, comb-like, through his beard. "All right, we'll try it," decided Booth. "Let's hire the dancing saloon."

"Hallelujah! Praise the Lord!" shouted Monk and Flawn, jumping up and dancing a jig of triumph before their amused leader.

So they held meetings in the dance hall every Sunday for several months, while the smaller weekday meetings were held in an old woolshed in Bethnal Green.

5

The Two Lieutenants

Many people thought George Scott Railton was mad. Though this was not true, he was extremely eccentric. By nature a loner, at nineteen he journeyed to Morocco as a missionary without support of any kind. This was in an age when the explorers of the Islamic African nations pretended to become Muslims to gain safe passage. He went to answer what he believed to be the call of God, but may just have been his own whim. He carried a banner inscribed in English, *Repentance—Faith—Holiness*. Needless to say, he met with no success, and with aid from the British Consul in Morocco and his elder brother in England, he returned to his homeland. It was a foolhardy and dangerous exploit, but it showed him to be a Christian soldier of action and courage.

A few years later, he saw advertised a booklet with the remarkable title, *How to Reach the Masses With the Gospel. A Sketch of the Origin, History and Present Position of the Christian Mission* (Booth's organization). Railton paid his sixpence and bought the booklet, which really *was* to be the call of God to him. He found it fascinating. Here was a man, William Booth, who really cared for the poor and the outcast. Here was a Christian who was able to reach them successfully in the name of Christ.

"While we highly esteem and regularly employ all accessory agencies," read Railton, tugging his wispy beard, "nevertheless, we place this first in the van, believing with Paul, that by the foolishness of preaching God has chosen to save them that believe. But how are they to be benefitted by preaching when, as we stated at the outset, the great bulk of the people cannot be

25

persuaded to set foot inside church, chapel, or preaching place of any kind? They cannot be saved by a Gospel that they do not hear. Feeling this, we go to them. Consequently, one of our principal spheres of labor is the 'open-air.' "

There was nothing new in that, it is true. Wesley and Whitefield, one hundred years before, had done the same thing; the Apostles, in the early days of Christianity, also took to the great outdoors. But as Railton read on the conviction grew that, "This man Booth has got it, and I, George Scott Railton, must join forces with him."

The tales of persecution, opposition, and mocking detailed in the pamphlet did nothing to put him off—indeed, they only strengthened his resolve. How could mud, stones, rotten eggs, and other missiles frighten a man who had tried to convert Muslim North Africa single-handed?

In March 1873 this enthusiastic Scotsman tied up the loose ends of his business commitments in Middlesborough and traveled to London to Booth's East End home in Gore Street, Hackney. The twenty-four-year-old had found the work which was to occupy the rest of his life.

The Rev. Launcelot Railton, George's elder brother, had contacted Booth and expressed concern about his brother's restlessness. Booth suspected that the younger Railton would be either a great help or a major hindrance to the mission. He took him into his own household, where he remained for eleven years as a welcome guest and tireless worker.

A crucial new worker from Booth's own family now joined the team—William Bramwell Booth—who, now aged seventeen, was beginning to shoulder a large amount of work. It was from this time that the mission began to grow rapidly, spearheaded by William, Senior, guided by Catherine, and organized by the two gifted "lieutenants," Railton and Bramwell.

The two young men hit it off immediately, becoming firm friends, and in spite of their relationship being clouded by frequent disagreement on policy, it lasted until Railton's death.

Bramwell had managed the "Food-for-the-Million" shops that his father had set up since he was sixteen years of age, and had shown himself unafraid of heavy responsibility. As a seven-year-old Bramwell had shocked his mother when she challenged him with the "offer of salvation in Christ." But a few weeks later the child was seeking forgiveness for his sins. From his early teens he accompanied his father in his evangelistic endeavors around the East End public houses, scarcely the ideal environment for a nervous, sickly youth.

"These are the people I want you to live and labor for, Willie," said the older Booth as they entered one tavern. "The poor have nothing but the public house."

The two wandered around the crowded bar, the father giving out tracts and talking to the men and women, some of whom were too drunk to have any idea what he was talking about. The son kept close to his father, watching and listening intently. "These are our people, son; our people. We must save them from the devil."

"Go home, you ravin' fool!" shouted a man leaning on the bar, "and take that skinny kid wiv yer." Jeers and yells arose in support of the mocking drunk.

"The Lord loves you and can rescue you from your wickedness," responded the elder Booth. "Come to the meeting at the New East London Theatre tomorrow night and be saved."

More jeers and boos greeted the evangelist's invitation. "You can have yer religion," shouted a man raising a glass above his head. "This is our religion!" Laughter and cheers greeted his statement.

The Booths quietly left the pub but William, turning as he did so, said, "Tomorrow night, then. Don't forget." A glass hurled through the closing doorway just missed Bramwell, and smashed as it hit the ground.

This was an unusual pastime for a thirteen-year-old but, inspired by the example of his father, William Bramwell Booth was also to become an evangelist. Like his parents, he also spent his life slaving for the poor, the underprivileged, and the unsaved.

The "Food-for-the-Million" shops were the Booths' first entry into the business-charity organizations with which the Salvation Army's name will always be associated. There were five such shops when Bramwell took over from Peter Monk in 1872. They were open twenty-four hours a day and catered especially to the poor, selling hot soup and a three-course meal for sixpence. These shops closed down in 1874, partly because some of the individual canteen managers objected to being answerable to the teenage Bramwell, and because William felt they had more important matters to attend to than fights over soup. But the younger Booth had proved himself to be an excellent administrator.

6

The Day of "Rest"

The Christian Mission's growing preaching stations were mainly in the East End area of London. The largest was the Whitechapel People's Mission Hall, a converted market that seated about 1,500 people. The cost of running the entire work was about £50 a week, but the offerings from all the stations totalled a mere £17 weekly. That gap of £33 was a continual anxiety to Booth, but with the aid of supporters, known and unknown, rich and poor, it was persistently bridged.

To Booth and his followers Sunday was the Lord's Day (Sabbath), but it was not a day of rest. No matter how hard they worked from Monday to Saturday, Sunday was the day when they slaved.

Catherine, with an energy that was surprising in one so frail and frequently indisposed, was up bright and early. Both she and her husband commenced the day with a time of private devotions. After this, with the help of the live-in maid, Jane Short, she began to organize the younger children for a day at the Mission. The children were dressed in their Sunday best—plain and cheap, but presentable, as befitted the children of a Christian preacher.

George Railton had already left the house, he was due to preach at one of the more distant halls, but an eight-mile hike both ways was not considered a hardship by this devoted man. Bramwell was due to take the morning service at another station, and was as usual rather nervous. Ballington, the sixteen-year-old second son of the Booths, was preparing to help another evangelist at the Bethnal Green hall. The rest of the children—Catherine, Emma, Herbert, Marian, Eva, and Lucy were to accompany their parents to the main mission hall.

The family arrived in good time for the seven o'clock prayer meeting with which each Lord's Day commenced. A surprisingly large group of the more faithful members had gathered to join them.

The meeting was led by Booth himself, as General Superintendent of the Christian Mission. He mounted the platform and raised his hand. The people quieted instantly.

"Brothers and sisters," he said softly, "as I was taking the Gospel around the public houses last night I was afraid. Afraid not of those people or of what they might do to me, but for them. I was afraid of the destruction to which their sinfulness will surely lead them if they do not turn to Christ.

"We have a responsibility to them. All of us earlier in our lives wasted our time in sinful pursuits. Many of us are no strangers to the demon drink. Like the prodigal son in our dear Lord's parable in Luke, chapter 15, they spend what they have in 'riotous living.' But our Heavenly Father seeks the fallen ones. He waits with open arms for sinners to come to Him. These people need our prayers. I urge you now to pray as you have never prayed before, and bring these dear men and women before our loving God."

Booth led in prayer, and various members of the assembly followed—not with eloquence, for these folk were not educated, but with sincerity. They prayed like publicans, not Pharisees. Loud amens punctuated the fervent prayers.

At eight o'clock the meeting was concluded, and followed by breakfast, tickets for which were threepence each. After breakfast more of the faithful drifted in—families, single men and women, all plainly and cheaply dressed, but surprisingly clean in a part of the world more noted for its dirt.

One of Booth's helpers ascended the platform stairs and began a simple homily on the need for holiness. He brought his address to a rather inconclusive end and invited others to share their thoughts on the subject. Several did, with keenness rather than depth.

Catherine, her long skirts rustling as she walked, left the building with the younger Catherine and Emma, leaving the rest of the children in Jane Short's charge. It was her task to preach to the amused well-to-do of London's West End. This was still an essential part of the mission's income, but Catherine did not just preach for money, for she knew well enough that the rich needed salvation every bit as much as the poor. In this ministry she met with considerably less success than her husband did at the other end of the economic scale, for "a rich man will find it hard to enter the kingdom of Heaven."

Back at the mission hall the crowd had now grown to well over two hundred, and they settled down for a further period of prayer. At the end of the prayer meeting Booth approached a giant of a man. "Dr. John," he said, "I want you to lead the open-air work this morning. There's been a lot of trouble lately and your presence might help to keep things quiet."

Dr. John Reid Morrison's heavily bearded face broke into a big smile. "You're right, Mr. Booth. Most of the locals seem a little wary of me," he said with delight, playfully aiming a punch at his leader. "Don't worry, I'll lead the march, and keep things peaceable."

At six foot three inches and 420 pounds, "Dr. John" was not a man easily intimidated, and though he was a gentle giant, his enormous bulk tended to threaten others.

Quickly the doctor rounded up some useful workers and, leaving the building, they went down the Whitechapel Road to the nearest public house. One of the women in the group played a concertina, leading the troops in a song:

> I will sing for Jesus,
> With His blood He bought me.

They were on the offensive, like good Christian soldiers.

The rest of the flock, further increased by a motley collection of people, commenced the morning service back at the People's Mission Hall.

The singing, led by one of Booth's assistants and accompanied by a woman on a rather battered piano, was rousing, yet rather discordant.

Later, Booth preached with fire. He knew no other way. His voice was strong, his manner earnest. At the end of the sermon they sang to the strains of the tune *Old Hundredth:*

> Just as I am without one plea,
> But that Thy blood was shed for me,

And that Thou bidd'st me come to thee,
O Lamb of God, I come, I come.

Without a word from Booth several people moved from various places around the building, some walking, others running, and fell on their knees at the little wooden benches situated in front of the platform. Quickly joined by mission workers, the seekers confessed their sins.

The gathering gradually broke up, and most made their way home. Others, with farther to travel, ate whatever lunch they had brought with them in the hall.

A smaller meeting took place in the afternoon, followed by a tea at threepence a head. That meal was succeeded by another prayer meeting, which in turn was followed by another venture into the streets. This time the aim was two-fold, to preach and to invite the lost back to the mission hall for the evening service. Three different groups, under the leadership of Monk, Morrison, and Booth, left the hall and went their separate ways.

Booth's contingent marched boldly down Whitechapel Road merrily singing:

Jesus, the name high over all,
In hell, or earth or sky.

Suddenly an enraged publican burst out of his hostel and hastened toward the singers, brandishing his fist. "'Ands off my customers, you ravin' lunatics! Go back to your b—'all!" he shouted.

Stirred by their host's action, a dozen of the pub's more aggressive patrons left their drinks and rushed at the procession. Violence—no stranger to the Salvationists—was still frightening, and the troops broke ranks and scattered every direction to avoid the attackers. One drunk, wielding a big stick, struck two of the male missioners viciously. One pressed his hand to the side of his face and fell to the ground. The other, holding his injured shoulder, moved quickly out of range. The other aggressors gestured threateningly and shouted abuse. Two of the Christians picked up their fallen comrade, and the whole party beat a tactical retreat, followed by a shower of stones and dirt from their tormentors. The drunks, their sport completed, returned to the pub laughing and cursing.

The danger over, Booth rallied his troops. A small group left the others and made their way back to the hall with the wounded men. The parade set off again, and the public wandering the streets or peering from the windows of the filthy homes were invited to the mission hall. Many came—young and old, men and women, poor and poorer followed the little army.

The evening meeting was due to begin. The atmosphere was electric in the crowded hall. The congregation of well over 1,000, which included an odd assortment of drunks, prostitutes, vagrants, and criminals, chattered and argued even after the service had started. As the meeting progressed the noise subsided slightly and Booth launched forth powerfully, denouncing sin and proclaiming his remedy for that sin, Jesus Christ. Even before he finished one woman fell to her knees, sobbing loudly. At the end of his address more people went on their knees seeking salvation.

The day of rest's work was nearly done. A final prayer meeting closed the day's activities, fifteen hours after they had begun. Booth was tired, but that was not unusual. Occasionally, by way of a change, he was totally exhausted.

The next morning George Railton was found asleep on top of the large boiler in the scullery. He had arrived home after everyone else had gone to sleep, and discovered that he did not have his key. Not wishing to wake the whole household by knocking on the door, he sneaked, thief-like, through a window with a faulty latch, and gained his well-earned rest on that unconventional bed. Railton, it was said, could sleep anywhere.

7

The Chimney-Sweep Evangelist

*E*leven years after Booth had commenced the work, another
key worker joined the growing ranks, named Elijah Cadman. Like so many of the early Salvationists, he was no
stranger to poverty. He was born in Coventry in 1843. His father
died when he was fifteen months old, and he was sent to work
in a factory at the age of five. A year later his mother, answering
an advertisement asking for "Small Boys for Narrow Flues," got
him a job climbing chimneys to clean them. His mother believed
he was especially suited for it, as he was very small, but strong.
He continued doing this until he was thirteen, when Lord Shaftesbury's law forbidding it began to take effect. He still cleaned
chimneys, using more civilized methods, and moved from Coventry to Rugby.

Elijah had been frequently drunk from the time he was six,
and in his new home earned himself a reputation as a hard drinker
and a tough fighter. He became friendly with a boxer and acted
as his sparring partner, even though he never quite attained the
height of five feet.

One Christmas they decided to celebrate the birth of the
Prince of Peace by going to see a public hanging. A little procession ascended the scaffold led by a chaplain, dressed in black,
with a prayer book in hand. Next came the condemned man,
followed by the executioner, also in black. At the sight of the
prisoner, a voice rose from the crowd, "Hats off!" and all the
men responded by uncovering their heads. A further shout rang

out from the rear of the throng, "Down in front!" and some at the front of the crowd crouched down to give those behind them a better view. The clergyman started to read aloud from his book. The executioner covered the victim's face and placed the noose around his neck, then went down the steps of the scaffold, paused for a moment and worked the trap. As the man fell, unseen by most of the crowd, another figure sprang and grasped the doomed man's legs, pulling until he was sure the poor wretch was dead.

Elijah and his friend had a fine view of the occasion, standing upon a large barrel. As they watched the body dangling from the gallows after the execution, the boxer turned to Cadman and said, "That's what you'll come to, 'Lijah, one day."

This struck the chimney-sweep like a bolt from the blue, and he hurriedly left the scene. Soon after this he gave up alcohol and tobacco.

Early one evening, the little Midland town of Lutterworth was alarmed by the sound of a handbell ringing. The little bell ringer, Elijah, stopped outside each inn and shouted in a loud, high-pitched voice, "This is to give notice that 60,000 people are lost. Lost! Lost! Lost! Lost, every year through the cursed drink. Mr. Cadman, the Sober Sweep, will give an account of his own drinking experience. Come and hear him! Come and hear him!" Clearly, a Salvationist in the making.

Sometime later he heard a street preacher, whose message threw him into a confused state of mind for several months. It was not relieved until one night he had a vision of Christ. He later recorded that sitting in his room, "My eyes were filled with tears and my heart of gladness." In his excitement, he ran downstairs and nearly tripped over another occupant of the house, and astonished her by shouting, "I've seen Jesus Christ!" He then ran down the street and told all those he met the same good news.

Cadman, as one would expect of a person who worked from the age of five, was illiterate. On one occasion he had the opportunity of reading the Bible at a meeting, which he did perfectly, except that he held it upside-down, blissfully unaware of the fact. Fortunately he had a good memory!

In 1865, the year of Booth's great decision, Cadman became convinced that God wanted him to get married. "The Lord told me I was to get married," he loved to tell. "So I said, 'Yes, Lord, when?' 'Next Christmas,' was the instruction. 'Yes, Lord,' " replied Elijah, as obedient as his biblical namesake. "In September, while I prayed the Lord reminded me that I was to be married at Christmas. I said, 'Lord, how can it be? I haven't got a girl yet!' "

The problem was solved through his job. A teacher at Rumba School asked him to clean his chimneys. On entering the house Elijah came face-to-face with a pretty servant, and it instantly struck him that this was the woman for him.

Not being a man to let the grass grow under his feet, when he got home he sent her a letter, dictated to a friend, proposing marriage. He received no reply.

Providentially, the schoolmaster's flues were proving really difficult, and Cadman was summoned to the house again. Again he met the attractive Maria Rosina.

"Good morning," he ventured.

"Good morning," came the courteous reply.

"Did you get a letter from me?"

"Yes."

"What did you think of it?"

"Nothing at all!" said the maid discouragingly.

"Well," said the sweep, "let me know 'yes' or 'no' by tomorrow morning's post. I can't stand waiting any longer." He turned and went about his business.

The letter came next day. It said, "Yes!"

They were duly married at Christmas, and spent fifty-seven happy though turbulent years together.

In 1876 Elijah—by then a Methodist lay preacher—and Maria heard of William Booth and the work of the Christian Mission. He felt compelled to go to London to meet this man.

He had become a fairly prosperous businessman, owning a shop in addition to his chimney sweep's concern. He entered the Whitechapel Road Mission Hall wearing a well-cut suit and a silk top hat. Small he may have been, but he stood out like a sore thumb.

He was interviewed by William, Bramwell, and Railton. Cadman was most impressed with what he saw and heard. The trio were less sure about him. "Would he be an asset or a liability to the Mission?" they wondered.

"Mr. Cadman," said the elder Booth, his gray eyes gazing intently at the prospective recruit, "we would like to give you opportunity to prove yourself. Would you be able to help in a revival meeting in Wellingborough this coming weekend?"

"Mr. Booth, I would be glad to 'elp you," the sweep replied.

That Saturday Elijah Cadman travelled to Wellingborough, another Midland town, and met with the Christian Mission staff there. The preparations for the meeting had all been made. It was Cadman's job to conduct the service that Sunday evening.

The evening came. The hall was crowded with the usual mixture of sinners and saints. Elijah led the singing enthusiastically and when he gave the address he launched forth on death, judgment, heaven and hell in a way that suggested he was familiar with them all, for he described them graphically. He even straddled the platform rail in a most precarious position, kicking legs and waving arms, to show how dangerous the spiritual condition was of those who wavered between Christ and the world.

William Booth, unknown to the little evangelist, was sitting in a room adjoining the main hall, listening to every word, though missing the dramatic visual effects.

Cadman learned of Booth's little deception later, and was delighted. The next day he escorted Booth to the railway station so that he could return to London. Just before the train's departure, Booth leaned through the carriage window and said, "Elijah Cadman, we need you. When can you come?"

"Whenever you like, Mr. Booth!" responded the delighted chimney sweep.

"Can you come in a fortnight?"

"Yes."

Elijah Cadman joined the staff of the Christian Mission on July 31, 1876.

8

Dowdle and His Violin

James Dowdle was six feet tall and strongly built, with a broad, open face and a boisterous character. He had worked for the railways as a guard and in later life even billed himself as "The Saved Railway Guard." But at the time of his meeting with Booth he was working for a builder called Stevens, doing a job for the Christian Mission—converting the Eastern Star public house into another mission hall.

Dowdle had had a religious experience through the ministry of an actor called John Hambleton and, though his interest in God waned for a time, it was rekindled at an open-air gathering led by his future employer, Stevens.

Stevens' daughter Claire, not a lady to be treated lightly, showed a certain amount of un-Victorian forwardness by inviting Dowdle to the People's Mission Hall to hear and meet William Booth. The thirty-five-year-old Dowdle and his future bride arrived at the hall just as the noisy parade was arriving for the evening service. Under his arm he carried his old violin.

"That one, no doubt, is Mr. Booth," observed Dowdle, pointing to the tall bearded figure at the head of the procession.

"Yes, that's Mr. Booth," his companion replied, "and a fine man he is too. Let's go in." They pushed through the jostling throng and entered the building.

The service began with the customary battle between pianist, song leader and singers, and the disruptive element that was part and parcel of the meetings. The pianist labored on her aged instrument, playing louder and louder in an effort to be heard above the racket.

Dowdle, always one to come to the aid of a lady in distress, pulled his violin from its battered case, rose and walked toward the platform, playing the hymn as he went. Momentarily the pianist, singers, and rabble-rousers quieted at this unexpected turn of events, but the missioners, quickly realizing that the violinist was an ally, picked up the tune again as Dowdle mounted the platform steps.

Each time the congregation sang, the ex-railway guard played with a vigor that excited the crowd, and he accompanied it with a little dance of feet surprisingly nimble for one so large.

When Booth preached James Dowdle sat enthralled. Gradually he realized that this man was no ordinary preacher, and that this night was no ordinary night. He decided that he must join Booth as a full-time worker, and that this young lady with him, if she felt the same way about the work, should become his wife.

After the service Booth made a beeline for the striking figure of Dowdle.

"This mission needs the likes of you," declared Booth.

"And I need the likes of this mission," chuckled James Dowdle.

"Then come and see me at my home at 3 Gore Road, Hackney, tomorrow night at seven o'clock, and we will discuss it," invited Booth.

"I'll be there, Mr. Booth. I'll be there."

Dowdle and Claire Stevens left the hall, and as they journeyed back to the Stevens' home, they both knew that life would never be the same again.

A few months later they were married and became part of Booth's expanding army. They were placed in charge of the Food Depot in Shoreditch, which they kept open from 5 A.M. to as late as 11 P.M. to sell food cheaply to the poor.

9

Illness Strikes

*I*f the year 1876 was a great one for gaining new recruits, especially two such as Cadman and Dowdle, it was certainly a disaster in other respects. Finance was a persistent problem, and the health of key workers—particularly the Booths—was terrible.

It began with Jane Short coming very close to a breakdown through overwork. Jane had gone to work for the Booths with considerable reservations. She feared that William and Catherine, whom she admired greatly, would not live up to the high principles they proclaimed from the pulpit. To her delight, for the most part they did, and she spent nine happy though hard-working years with them.

Miss Short found that at times William could be bad-tempered, particularly when suffering from a bout of dyspepsia, a complaint which later became chronic. Yet his bad moods did not last long, and in a moment he could change from gloom to hilarity. Also she believed that Booth (who firmly advocated the maxim, "Spare the rod, spoil the child") was too harsh with the children. This was no doubt true, but the children loved him, though perhaps not as tenderly as they loved their mother. They called him "The Bishop."

Catherine—austere yet sweet-natured—was also a strict disciplinarian. But, as her eldest son was to reflect years later, her insistence on her children being obedient was "not derived from the fact that obedience in children was more comfortable for the grown-up; it was her appreciation of the fact that obedience was a necessary principle in education, growth, and development."

She was, Jane Short discovered, as passionately concerned about people as her dedicated husband.

"Sister" Jane, because of her sickness, departed on a sea cruise, that Victorian cure for all ills. Her exit from the Booth household may well have saved her life. Her successor, Mary, was not so fortunate.

If Jane Short was brought to ill-health through overwork, she was just following the example of the Booth family. Bramwell, by no means physically strong, had heart trouble that year as well as a worsening of his hearing problem, but worked as hard as ever. William Booth caught gastric fever, and after nursing him Catherine had a breakdown. As a girl she had suffered from consumption, which left her with poor health, and she was still afflicted with curvature of the spine.

Then Mary, the maid, became sick with smallpox and died. Lucy, the youngest of the Booth family, and Railton both caught the disease but recovered.

The sickness of the Mission's leaders and William and Catherine's departure to convalesce on the south coast not unnaturally caused serious problems. On his return to London Booth was faced with resignations from several senior workers because of ill health, dissatisfaction with the running of the work and, in the case of two women, marriage. The leaders of the Poplar Station, where Railton was evangelist, had sent a letter to Booth requesting Railton's removal.

The General Superintendent, who was never one to smile on fighting in the ranks when there was a deadly enemy to contend with, smoothed over the Poplar trouble with a visit and some stern words. Reorganization and new appointments solved the other difficulties.

10

The Dowdles in Action

James and Claire Dowdle, after their breaking-in period as mission workers at Shoreditch, were moved to Chatham, Leeds, and Bradford in quick succession, conducting a string of evangelistic meetings.

One cold Saturday afternoon at the end of 1876, Dowdle was walking down a Bradford street, merrily swinging his umbrella. As he went he stopped and talked to anyone he could, urging those who would listen to consider their spiritual condition, and giving out leaflets advertising his meetings. One of the recipients was a well-built teenage boy with a broad face, called John Lawley. John was the son of a poverty-stricken farm worker, who had moved to Bradford in hope of improving his circumstances. But his father, by then employed as a laborer, only managed to eke out an existence for his family of twelve.

"Eh, what's it about then, mister?" queried the lad as Dowdle handed him a handbill.

"It's an invitation to come to the mission hall just down the road tonight, son, to hear about the Lord Jesus," said James, pointing his umbrella toward the hall two hundred yards away. "We're fighting a war, my boy. We're fighting a war for God," he challenged.

"I might just do that too, mister," responded the boy.

"Do come. Make sure you come," urged the smiling preacher, playfully stabbing the younger man with his umbrella.

Dowdle turned and approached a group standing at a fish and vegetable stall, inspecting the owner's wares. The evangelist started giving his leaflets to these folk with an eager, verbal invitation to the weekend's rallies.

The man came out from behind his stall, objecting to his potential customers being sidetracked. He grabbed Dowdle—big man as he was—by his coat front and waved a threatening fist in his face. "Push off, and leave me customers alone before I blacks yer eye."

Dowdle, not wishing for a fight when on the Lord's business, knew that he must back down. "Yes, of course. But here's a leaflet for you," he offered.

The man shoved the ex-railway guard away with a growl of anger. "Get out of 'ere and take yer b— pieces of paper with yer." He returned to his stand, stocked with its meager supply of fish and vegetables, and continued his sales patter to the little group who had watched the encounter in amused silence.

That evening John Lawley accepted the invitation and visited the mission hall. He had never seen anything like it in his life. Dowdle, prancing around the stage, played his "Hallelujah Fiddle" to accompany the songs, while his wife led the meeting. When things got too noisy James would blow on an old whistle, as in his railway days, in a not always successful attempt to silence the throng.

During the singing of one song, Claire left the platform to deal with a lout who was continually disrupting the meeting. She walked down the aisle between the wooden benches, went around behind him and grabbed him by the coat collar. She pressed her knuckles firmly in the back of the offender's neck and, as he stood up, pushed him in the direction of the door. With a final shove, the crestfallen troublemaker was propelled through the exit with surprising force. The congregation erupted in a mixture of laughter and cheers.

As the noise gradually subsided, James Dowdle seized his opportunity and began to preach. Warnings about fire and brimstone issued forth from his lips, his countenance taking on an unusually stern appearance. At the end of his discourse a sobbing John Lawley came forward to trust in Christ. From then on he worked for the Christian Mission, becoming its fortieth full-time evangelist.

11

Booth's Autocracy

Since 1870 the affairs of the Christian Mission had been governed by the Annual Conference, which was modelled on the Methodist Church pattern. These conferences were attended by all full-time evangelists on the mission staff and two elected lay delegates from each mission station. The original doctrines and disciplines of the mission were adopted at the first conference. In 1875 a new set of rules, much shorter than the previous one, was introduced. The year 1876 was to see the largest and last conference, with 67 men and women present.

This system of government, though in theory democratic, was less so than its Methodist counterpart. As George Railton wrote later, "What was done or not done during the year had little or no connection with any resolution of the conference itself." In other words the conferences were a waste of valuable time, and discontent with this method of administration was increasing, particularly with Railton and Bramwell.

William was not happy with the situation either, but was wary of the suggested alternative—to make him the man to give the orders and everybody else in the organization subject to those commands. Autocracy was the answer, and Booth was by nature autocratic, but he hesitated from taking that step. Yet how could a war—and make no mistake, they were fighting a war—be run by a committee?

As the year 1877 dawned a meeting took place which, though small, was to lead to a gigantic change of policy. Railton, Bramwell, and a few other leaders selected by them approached Booth. They explained that they did not want a democracy—they wanted a dictatorship, for they believed they had nothing to fear from a dictator as benevolent as William Booth.

Bramwell concluded their case: "Father, we did not give ourselves to form a little church as an appendix of Methodism. We gave ourselves to you to be guided by you."

Booth was anxious, for the way ahead was not clear. Autocracy was appealing to him, but the responsibility of it disturbed him. Was he so close to God that he could be sure that his decisions were always right? Did it matter? For surely no committee could infallibly make the right choices either.

He asked the group to leave the matter for a while and to pray about it.

In May an article written by Booth appeared in *The Christian Magazine*. It left little doubt as to what would happen:

> There have been more than enough conferences, and congresses, and committees and deliberations. It is time to act. There is not a moment to lose. There cannot be any question about what we have to do. No more conferences! No more doubt! No more delay! Arise, ye children of the light, and buckle on the armor bright, and now prepare yourselves to fight against the world and Satan. We are called to be saints. We are called to be brothers and sisters of Jesus, to fight with him, for him, with every particle of strength we have to the last gasp. That is enough. No more conference!

The last conference in June enthusiastically agreed to his proposals for a reorganization of the mission under his direct superintendency.

Democracy came to an end for the lifespan of William Booth in the organization which was to become the Salvation Army. There was little objection among the Christian Mission staff. Some, like Dowdle, had doubts about it, but most were relieved and delighted. The majority of those who would have opposed this autocratic form of government had already left the organization, no doubt seeing the direction in which it was moving.

Part 2

The Army

12

The Salvation Army Is Born

*I*n Yorkshire's coastal town of Whitby in November 1877 appeared numerous posters:

WAR! WAR! IN WHITBY 2,000 MEN AND WOMEN
Wanted at once to join the Hallelujah Army
That is making an attack on the devil's kingdom
every Sunday in ST. HILDA'S HALL
at 11 A.M., 3 and 6.30 P.M.
And every week night in the Old Town Hall at 7:30
To be led by CAPTAIN CADMAN from London,
Evangelist of the Christian Mission.

Christian Mission it may still have been, but with words like "War," "Hallelujah Army," "attack" and "Captain," a military-style organization was emerging.

Another sign for the same campaign read:

THE MIDDLESBRO ARTILLERY
Is to arrive at 9:30 A.M. with the big guns. After the morning conflict a public ham-sandwich tea will be provided in the Congress Hall at 3 o'clock. Tickets 9d each.
At 6:30 the army will muster again on the Pier, and after a

short fight will march to the Congress Hall, which is the
HOSPITAL FOR THE WOUNDED

Not many armies would have held a ham-sandwich tea while on active duty, but the Christian Mission was quickly becoming an army. The military terminology had been creeping in for some time, encouraged by the stories of the warriors of the Old Testament and verses in the New Testament such as the apostle Paul's instruction to Timothy, "Fight the good fight of faith." In this Cadman was the main innovator, the various military titles and phrases usually being introduced by him.

The General Superintendent was increasingly having his title shortened to General, a practice which had begun with the Booth family purely as shorthand for the original title, but which became more widespread as the martial thinking developed. During Cadman's Whitby crusade Booth told him he would pay the town a visit, and on hearing this Elijah flooded the area with leaflets advertising the arrival of "the General of the Hallelujah Army."

In May 1878 Bramwell and Railton were summoned to Booth's bedroom to go through a proof of the mission's annual report. Booth, recovering from sickness and looking pale and drawn, walked the floor dressed in a yellow dressing-gown. The report, compiled by Railton as secretary of the mission, was headed:

THE CHRISTIAN MISSION
under the Superintendence
of the Rev. William Booth
is

A VOLUNTEER ARMY

The Volunteer Army of that time was a civilian army which had been consistently ridiculed by the magazine *Punch*. Bramwell looked at the first page of the report, frowned and said disapprovingly, "Volunteer Army? George, I'm not a volunteer, I'm a regular or nothing."

Railton looked at his friend, smiled, and shrugged his shoulders as if to say, "Well, what should it be then?" but remained silent.

Booth, meanwhile, had stopped pacing the room; his fingers slowly stroked his beard as he thought for a moment. Then it struck him like a bolt from the blue. He stepped toward the table on which the proof lay. He snatched up a pen, crossed out the word "Volunteer" and substituted "Salvation." Railton and Bramwell, sitting at the table, peered at their leader's alteration on the paper in front of them, and, almost as one, leaped from their chairs.

"Thank God for that!" exclaimed the younger Booth.

"Praise the Lord!" shouted the excited Railton as he jumped up and down on the spot. "Salvation Army! That's what we are, a Salvation Army!"

The three men looked at one another, their smiles turned into laughter, and they laughed and laughed until the tears ran down their cheeks.

In September *The Christian Mission Magazine* reported on a War Congress held in London. The account stated that the mission had "organized a Salvation Army to carry the blood of Christ and the fire of the Holy Ghost into every corner of the world." Also in that edition of the magazine William Booth was described as the General, and this was to become more and more common that year.

As late as December, Booth still had reservations about his new title. On Christmas Eve he wrote to his eldest son on the new headed notepaper printed for his organization. The heading was:

THE SALVATION ARMY
called The Christian Mission

General WILLIAM BOOTH

Headquarters,
272 Whitechapel Road, London

Booth had circled the word "General" and written at the top of the sheet, "Can't this form be altered? It looks so pretentious."

Pretentious or not, Booth was now the General of the Salvation Army, and his troops made sure that there was no going back. On the first day of 1879 the organization officially changed its name.

Also in January their monthly publication, *The Christian Mission Magazine* underwent a name change and became *The Salvationist.* In it the General penned an article entitled, *Our New Name.* He wrote:

Only the name—the same old friend, neither altered in dress or person, bringing the same message at the same intervals—only a more expressive appellation and a more descriptive one, for in deed and truth has not our paper always been an exponent, advocate, and record of Salvation?

We are a Salvation people—this is our specialty—getting saved and keeping saved, and then getting somebody else saved, and then getting saved ourselves more and more, until full salvation on earth makes the heaven within.

WE BELIEVE IN SALVATION. We believe in the old-fashioned salvation. We have not developed and improved into Universalism, Unitarianism, or Nothingarianism, or any other form of infidelity, and we don't expect to. Ours is just the same salvation taught in the Bible, proclaimed by Prophets and Apostles, preached by Luther and Wesley and Whitefield, sealed by the blood of martyrs—the very same salvation that was purchased by the sufferings and agony and blood of the Son of God.

We believe the world needs it; this and this alone will set the world right. We want no other nostrum—nothing new. We are on the track of the old Apostles. You don't need to mix up any other ingredients with the heavenly remedy. Wound and kill with the old sword, and pour in the old balsam and you will see the old result—Salvation. The world needs it. The worst man that ever walked will go to Heaven if he obtains it, and the best man that ever lived will go to Hell if he misses it. Oh, publish it abroad!

There is a Hell. A Hell as dark and terrible as is the description given of it by the lips of Jesus Christ, the Truthful. And into that Hell men are departing hour by hour. While we write men are going into everlasting punishment. While we eat and drink, sleep and work, and rest, men are going where the worm dieth not, and where the fire is not quenched.

So wake up all the powers of your being, my brothers, and consecrate every awakened power to the great end of saving them. Be a Salvationist.

Oh, for a brave year. We shall have one, and you will fight and drive the foe, and rescue the prey, and we will enter the record of multitudes rescued and saved and sanctified and safe landed in Glory in the pages of the *Salvationist.*

The magazine may not have altered in dress, but very soon the Army's male soldiers were to do so, by donning red jerseys as a uniform. The females were initially less keen to take the new name that literally, and it was over a year before the Booths themselves followed the example of their male subordinates.

13

"Gypsy" Smith

The Gypsies have been a very visual part of British life for generations. Their nomadic lifestyle fit well with the fairground activities from which most of them earned their living. Their aloofness and insistence upon marriages with their own kind gave them, like the Jews, a distinct identity. It was from their ranks that another Salvationist emerged, Rodney "Gypsy" Smith. The golden-voiced Smith was later to secede from the Army and become to Britain, between the two World Wars, what Billy Graham was to be to America and the world for a later generation.

His first appointment as an officer in the Salvation Army was at Chatham in Kent. His welcome there was not very encouraging, as the soldiers there protested that he was too young to lead them. He was young, as were most of the other officers, but his beardless face made him look younger than he really was. He responded to their criticism with faultless logic, "I may be young, but if you let me stay a while, I shall get older."

He was transferred to the mill town of Bolton in Lancashire, to serve with an ex-laborer, William Corbridge. One evening Gypsy ventured forth with John Davey to preach the Gospel in the stone-house-lined streets. Corbridge was sick and unable to go with them. They stood on a street corner opposite a public house and preached to the numerous men and women wandering about. A crowd began to gather, and as its size increased its mood worsened. At first the people were content just to shout insults, but when they tired of that they began to throw stones. The two Salvationists soldiered bravely on in spite of the opposition, but the mob, angry at its lack of success, rushed at Davey and Gypsy, sweeping them literally off their feet. The rabble went down the street with the two evangelists lost in the midst of it. They both knew their lives were in danger if they did not escape and, almost miraculously, by pushing and struggling they worked their way through the mob who, in the poor light and chaotic conditions, were unable to identify them clearly. They broke through the confines of the jostling crowd and ran home as fast as they could.

The next evening Corbridge decided to join them, even though there was no improvement in his health. They walked to the site of the previous day's dangers accompanied by a handful of helpers, including a short but strongly built sweep named Jim Johnson. Corbridge, standing on tottery legs and shaking visibly, opened the meeting, exhorting his listeners to repent. The crowd gathered even more quickly than on the night before, and their mood proved to be just as black.

For the second successive occasion the mob rushed at the Salvationists. Having learned their lesson from the previous evening, the little army decided to beat a hasty retreat. Johnson and Gypsy brought up the rear, while the others hurried ahead as best they could with the ailing Corbridge. As the ringleaders of the rabble caught up with Smith and Johnson, a man aimed a blow with a stick at Gypsy. Before the implement landed, Johnson punched the assailant hard in the stomach and he fell in a crumpled heap at the sweep's feet. At the unexpected turn of events the mob's forward surge momentarily ceased, which gave the evangelists opportunity to take refuge in a chemist's shop owned by a sympathizer.

The crowd recovered its sense of purpose and continued to pursue its quarry. They assembled outside the little shop, screaming and shouting. But before the mob could decide its next move a group of eight or nine policemen arrived on the scene. The senior constable entered the chemist's while his companions tried to quiet the noisy mob.

"Are you gentlemen all uninjured?" asked the policeman.

"Yes, thank God!" replied Gypsy.

"I think me and my men 'ad better escort you 'ome," suggested the constable.

"We don't want to go 'ome yet. We want to preach the

Gospel," said a defiant Corbridge.

"That's not wise, sir. The mob is out for blood, and though I've more officers on the way, I cannot guarantee your safety."

"Nevertheless, we must preach. Would you be good enough to accompany us to the town square?" asked Corbridge.

"You really shouldn't go, sir."

"But we must! If you don't go with us we will go on our own. These people need the Gospel," persuaded the sick Salvationist.

The policeman considered the matter for a moment, then said, "We will leave by the back door. Let's be quick about it."

So the group, escorted by the officer of the law, left the relieved chemist and walked speedily to the square. Their departure was not noticed immediately, but the word of their appearance in the square reached the growing crowd who proceeded to move to the new scene of activity.

Since Corbridge was too ill to continue, this time Gypsy Smith was preaching, and his strong mellow voice carried above the din. The police, their numbers doubled, kept the crowd at a safe distance. When Gypsy concluded, the policemen, their ranks now further increased, escorted the evangelists away from the still angry mob.

14

Progress, North and South

*L*ouisa Lock was fourteen years old when she first joined the Christian Mission, and she became an evangelist two years later. At the end of 1878, by then an eighteen-year-old officer in the Salvation Army, she was sent north with five other young women to start the work in Durham and Northumberland, farther north than the Army had ever ventured before. She served at the coastal towns of Sunderland and Seaham before venturing inland to Gateshead, while others in her party crossed the River Tyne and took the good news to Newcastle.

That winter was long and very cold. The petite Louisa was not afraid of poor conditions, but she virtually abandoned the open-air work as the weather reached its zenith. Not only had standing in the open in the snow and blustery, icy north winds damaged her health but few, at times none, were willing to stand to listen in such bitter conditions.

Louisa discovered, however, that her little hall in Gateshead was becoming a focal point for those looking for warmth and friendship. Though there was not always enough coal to keep their fire burning, in spite of the surrounding coalfields, the numerous human bodies warmed the room.

The work was proving successful in most of the new northern outposts, and as spring finally dawned, strongholds had been firmly established in Sunderland, Gateshead, and Newcastle. In May, William and Catherine Booth traveled north to join their front-line troops in Tyneside to hold a council of war. A crowd of about 4,000 gathered at the Newcastle Circus. The fast-growing use of uniforms was most evident, though the Booths still declined to wear them. Many of the soldiers wore red jerseys, while others sported red armbands, or had red handkerchiefs around their necks.

Catherine was to present the newly designed Salvation Army flags, red and blue with a yellow sun centerpiece, to the new corps that had been established through the zeal of Louisa Lock and her energetic colleagues.

Dressed in a somber brown, full-length dress, with a shawl held tightly around her and a bonnet tied under her chin, Catherine walked to the front of the platform and raised a delicate hand. The cheering crowd quieted with an air of expectancy.

In a gentle but surprisingly powerful voice she said, "Dear brothers and sisters in Christ, this is a great day in the story of our noble little army. A day on which we can recognize with praise that much has been achieved for our Lord Jesus Christ. But we must not be complacent! The world is suffering. The world is lost.

"The time has come," she said with growing fervor, "for fire. All other agents have been tried: intellect, learning, fine buildings, wealth, respectability, numbers. The great men and the mighty men and the learned men have all tried to cast out these devils before you, and have failed. Try the fire!

"There are legions of the enemies of our great King. Fire on them. There are the legions of strong drink, damning millions; of uncleanness, damning millions more; of debauchery, blasphemy, theft, millions more. Charge on them; pour the red-hot shot of the artillery of heaven on them," she said with vigor, "and they will fall by thousands!"

Another cheer went up, but she continued, touching the flag nearest to her. "The flag is a symbol of our devotion to our great Captain, and to the great purpose for which He shed His blood, that He might redeem men and women from sin and death and hell. This flag is emblematical of our faithfulness to our great trust. Jesus only wants faithful soldiers in order to win the uttermost parts of the earth for His possession. If Christian soldiers had been faithful in the past, the world would have been won for Christ long ago.

"This flag, though, is an emblem of victory," she emphasized, as again the crowd roared. "By what power is that victory going to be achieved? By fire! The Holy Ghost! This fire of the Spirit can transform us as it did Peter. Let all go that occupies the room which the Holy Ghost might fill in your souls. Charge on the hosts of hell, and see whether they will not turn and flee," she concluded in triumph. Once more the people burst into cheering.

Catherine Booth took the flags one by one and presented them to the proud captains. Louisa Lock mounted the platform last, and when she was handed the symbolic standard, she waved it enthusiastically, to the delight of the throng.

The following year Louisa married another Salvation Army officer. The year after that, she died of tuberculosis, not having reached her twenty-first birthday.

With the rapid spread of the work William and Catherine found themselves together less often. After a council of war, the General returned to his headquarters in Whitechapel, while his wife undertook a campaign of quite a different sort in Bournemouth on the south coast.

Her hostess was Lady Cairns, who had heard Catherine preach several times in London's West End and admired her greatly. Her Ladyship had arranged for the Salvationist to take a service on a Saturday night in a hall at the seaside resort. But she was most concerned about the questionable etiquette of one of the Salvation Army's practices, which might invade the Bournemouth meeting.

"Mrs. Booth," said her Ladyship over tea on the Friday afternoon. "I hope you are not going to . . . ask people out."

"Ask people out? To the penitent form, do you mean?" questioned Catherine.

"Yes, Mrs. Booth," she confirmed, "asking people out to the, er . . . penitent form is not a good idea in Bournemouth. Our people here are rather proud, I'm afraid. More tea?"

Catherine declined, and her Ladyship continued. "No one will come out if you do—they are too proud, you see—and it might prejudice people against you and the Gospel. People here are quite different from those in the East End of London."

Catherine hesitated for a moment, not because of doubts about her intentions, but rather because she needed to select the correct words carefully. "Your Ladyship, you are right that the men and women of Bournemouth are very different from those in London's East End." Her Ladyship smiled at the concession, but Catherine carried on speaking. "But one thing all people have in common, rich or poor, of high or low estate, is that they are all sinners. The apostle Paul in his Epistle to the Romans tells us that 'all have sinned, and come short of the glory of God.' He does not distinguish between rich and poor. All need to repent!"

"Yes, Mrs. Booth, I do agree, but our people here are not used to this sort of thing. I do not believe that any will come out," warned her Ladyship earnestly.

"Your Ladyship, I believe I have no alternative. I dare not preach without an appeal and, whether the folk of Bournemouth are proud or not, I will ask them out, and I will leave the consequences to God," said the preacher.

Lady Cairns looked perplexed, but knew there was no point in asking Catherine Booth to preach unless she was able to do so with freedom. "Well, Mrs. Booth, if you must, then you must. I hope you will not be disappointed."

"No, your Ladyship, I don't think I will be," said Catherine confidently.

The Saturday night meeting commenced. The hall was packed with the "proud" men and women of Bournemouth. The audience was far more sedate and subdued than those usually addressed by a Salvationist. The singing, accompanied by a gentleman on a grand piano, was more melodious than one would expect at the Whitechapel Mission Hall. The prayers were led by a local clergyman and were not greeted with shouts of "Amen" and "Praise the Lord," as they would have been at a corps in Hackney. When Catherine rose to speak, hers was the only voice heard. There were no cries of "Hallelujah" in support of her words, and no calls of derision from those who may have opposed her message.

She concluded her sermon, "But what was it Jesus did? He lived, labored, wept, suffered, and died and atoned for me, and He did it all till He cried, 'It is finished!' But I nowhere read that He 'repented' and 'turned to God' and did 'works meet for repentance' and 'obeyed the Gospel' for me. This He commands every soul to do for itself, or perish."

Her body was quivering with emotion as she finished the address. She then announced the final hymn and appealed to sinners to come out and kneel in repentance. As the hymn was sung, twelve proud people of Bournemouth did come out, to her Ladyship's surprise and relief!

15

The War Cry
and a Pea-Souper

As 1879 drew to a close it became clear to the General and his senior officers that their monthly paper, *The Salvationist,* was inadequate. What was needed was a weekly publication. Bramwell and Railton, two of the most literate of Army members, spent much of December planning the new venture. On Christmas Day, Railton celebrated Christ's birth by finishing the preparation of the material for the printer, Captain William Pearson.

On Friday, Boxing Day, Railton caught an early train to go north, where he was to conduct a campaign, leaving the Booths and Pearson at the mercy of a secondhand, gas-engined printing press that refused to cooperate. They labored throughout the day, at times coaxing, at others battling the unmanageable machine, which was tearing up most of the papers it printed. At times it stopped altogether.

At 11 P.M. when they finally gave up and brought in a repairman, they had successfully printed a mere two hundred saleable copies of their new paper. They went home for a short night's rest and returned early the next morning to the printing offices, through a slight fog, to discover that the mechanic had done an excellent job. The press now worked, and was printing papers at 1,400 an hour. But the previous day's hold-ups had put them behind schedule. Apart from doing deliveries of the paper to the local mission halls, it was also necessary to take the bundles of papers to the main line railway stations, so that they could be forwarded to the outposts scattered throughout the country.

As afternoon came the fog developed into a typical London "pea-souper," and the Salvationists worried that their valiant attempts to meet the deadline would be thwarted by the inclement weather.

The General limped over to the window—he had hurt his leg in a fall at Preston railway station two weeks before—and peered out into the gloom of fog-bound Fieldgate Street. "How can we possibly get these papers to the railway stations in these conditions?" he said.

"We could get a cab, General," suggested Pearson.

"But how would you find a cabbie in this?" asked Booth, casting another look outside.

"I'll give it a try," volunteered Bramwell. He pulled on his coat and ventured out into the unpleasant weather.

"God bless you, Bramwell. We pray that you'll find one," encouraged Booth.

Bramwell left the printery and slowly walked in the direction of the city of London, which he knew would be the most likely place to find a hansom. He inched his way along in the declining visibility; and eventually found a cab by Aldgate Pump.

"Cabbie!" he called. "I've an urgent job for you."

"I was thinking about calling it a day, guv. This fog is bad, and it's getting worse all the time. Where did you want to go?" responded the cab driver.

For the first time the difficulty of his task dawned upon him. "Well," hesitated Bramwell, "I've got some parcels to despatch by rail."

"Which station, guv?"

Bramwell looked at the man sheepishly and said, "Kings Cross and . . . er . . . St. Pancras, Euston, Paddington, and Waterloo."

The driver's jaw dropped as he heard the list of destinations. "In these conditions, guv'nor? We'll never make it."

"It's the Lord's work, friend. Please help. It is very important," beseeched Bramwell.

The cabbie thought for a moment and, with a shrug of his shoulders, consented. "As you please, guv. Which one first?"

Bramwell, climbing aboard, said, "Well, first we need to pick up the parcels from the printery in Fieldgate Street, Whitechapel."

The cabbie's mouth opened again in amazement at the un-expected extension of the trip. Bramwell sat down in the cab. Visibility was so poor that the driver, high on his seat at the back, could only see the rear end of his horse; but with a crack of his whip he moved the animal off slowly, in the direction of the White-chapel printing shop.

They arrived at Fieldgate Street, where the driver helped the Salvationists load the passenger section of his cab with the bun-dled papers. The press was still printing further copies of the new paper for the London Citadels, which would be delivered on foot, fog or no fog.

The hansom, with Bramwell on board again, moved in the direction of Kings Cross station. By this time the unseen sun was setting, worsening visibility still further.

Slowly they journeyed down Pentonville Road when, with a sudden jolt, the left-hand wheel of the hansom mounted the pave-ment. Before the driver could direct the horse and cab back on to the road they came to an unexpected halt as the wheel collided with a lamppost. The impact made a fearful clang.

"Whoa," called the driver, reining the horse in. He climbed down to inspect the damage, and the worried Bramwell joined him.

"Any damage done?" asked the Salvationist.

The driver was looking anxiously at his source of livelihood. "Nothing serious, guv. Let's give it another try."

After three hours of tortuously slow driving through the Lon-don streets, the precious parcels were left at the five main line railway stations, and dispatched to their destinations.

The cabbie returned his passenger to the printery and Bram-well reached up and shook the driver warmly by the hand. "God bless you. God bless you. The soldiers of the Salvation Army thank you for your help. How much do I owe you?"

"What about five bob, guv?" suggested the driver.

Bramwell reached into his pocket and pulled out the coins and gave them to the man. "Thank you again," he said appreciatively.

"Bye, guv'nor. I think I will call it a day now," said the cabbie with a grin. He pulled off and vanished in the fog. The clopping of the horse's hooves continued well after the hansom was no longer visible.

The new paper went on sale that night in the London Citadels of the Salvation Army, and some soldiers even ventured into the pubs to sell the first edition of *The War Cry* at a halfpenny each. The leading article read:

> Why a weekly *War Cry?* Because the Salvation Army means more war. No more surrender; no more truce; no more inactivity as to sin and ruin. No more sin! Bought with blood, Israel is to be cleansed with that blood; and to be kept separate and unspotted from the world.
>
> Then on to victory! Let every faint heart be strong. Our eyes have seen His salvation. The very salvation that gladdens our hearts has come wherever we have fought. Aha, we shall conquer! To that end let *The War Cry* go everywhere! Quick!

Under a heading, *Seize North Wales!* came this exchange:

The General, headquarters, to Railton:

> "I authorize you to raise a special force for the salvation of Wales, to be called the Mountaineers, on the terms you propose, to commence by seizing the counties of Flint and Denbigh as soon as possible. Go ahead! The Lord help you."

Railton to General:

> "Thanks. Have already 20 volunteers eager for marching orders. Hope soon for 200 from which to select sufficient to sweep the Principality. Shall hold first review of volunteers, Bethnal Green, Saturday afternoon, January 10, 1880, three o'clock."

16

The Invasion of America

*B*efore January had run its course Railton's talent became needed in another, much larger country—America.

In an age of emigration it was inevitable that some of Booth's followers would travel to other lands. In the Christian Mission days, back in 1872, James Jermy emigrated from Whitechapel to Cleveland, Ohio and helped to organize a Christian work there based on the pattern of Booth's mission in England.

While wandering through the poorer areas of Cleveland, Jermy saw a building with a sign outside that read, *Christian Chapel. The Poor Have the Gospel Preached Unto Them.* Jermy, attracted by its apparent similarity to Christian Mission buildings, entered the Chapel and discovered a small group of black people under the leadership of James Fackler. The two men liked each other instantly, so the Englishman decided to join forces with his newfound brethren. Jermy told Fackler stories of William Booth's work in London and he was so impressed that he agreed that Jermy should write to Booth for advice, and for permission to bring their Chapel under the wing of the Christian Mission.

The letter arrived while Booth was suffering a long bout of sickness, and it was more than six months before Booth's affirmative reply was forthcoming. The mission in Cleveland progressed, and in 1873 a second station was opened. However, when Jermy returned to England the following year the organization severed its connection with the Christian Mission.

In April 1878 a Salvationist from Coventry, Amos Shirley, emigrated to Philadelphia and started work in a silk factory. Sixteen months later, when he had established himself, he sent for his wife Anna and teenage daughter Eliza to join him. Eliza was already a lieutenant in the Salvation Army.

They decided to start the work of the Salvation Army in Philadelphia. They rented an old chair factory on the corner of Sixth and Oxford Streets and named it "The Salvation Factory." The strategy of the parent body in England was followed, and open-air meetings and marches became a prominent feature of their activities. They quickly attracted attention and gained numerous converts.

As the work developed, Anna and Eliza often led most of the open-air gatherings while Amos organized the services back in their meeting place. Mother and daughter, both dressed entirely in black, and supported by a little band of helpers, preached and led the singing in Philadelphia's streets.

Early in 1880 the Shirleys had to rent a second hall, as their Salvation Factory was too small to accommodate all those wishing to attend, even though it held about 1,000.

They had previously informed Booth of their work, but he had been reluctant to recognize their efforts as officially part of the Salvation Army. The experience with Jermy and Fackler had disappointed him, and he was dubious about other such endeavors. But as further reports came with requests for help, Booth came to realize the potential and decided to organize an invasion force under the leadership of Railton.

Railton's first task was to select his soldiers for the attack on the United States. He carefully chose Captain Emma Westbrook, aged thirty-three, and six teenage "Hallelujah Lasses"—Rachel Evans, Clara Price, Mary Coleman, Elizabeth Pearson, Annie Shaw, and Emma Morris.

Nearly a hundred years before, England had failed to hold on to its American colonies with trained troops. Now a General with quite a different mission was sending an army of eight, six under the age of twenty, to capture America for God.

On Thursday, February 12, 1880, an official farewell began at Headquarters in Whitechapel with a tea. The building was attractively decorated with banners, streamers, and posters, and was packed with over 500 soldiers and various dignitaries.

George Railton had originally had reservations about the use of a uniform. He was afraid that it might erect a barrier between the Army and those it sought to save, but on this occasion he became the first to wear a full Salvation Army uniform. It consisted of navy blue trousers and coat, the coat with a high-fitting collar and almost entirely hiding the now familiar red jersey. The collar sported a red badge with a yellow *S* emblazoned on it.

The women too were in full uniform, with ankle-length navy dresses and loose-fitting, thigh-length coats buttoned to the collar and trimmed with red. Their hats (bonnets were to come later) were like a shortened version of the English policeman's helmet, encircled by a red band with the words *The Salvation Army* in yellow.

The General addressed the enthusiastic gathering. "This is our first venture into foreign parts, but it will not be our last. Already I have an invitation"—he waved a piece of paper in the air—"to invade France. We have a precious request to go to Sweden, and we already have one Swedish captain ready trained. Then there is Germany, and that great country Russia that I long for us to get into. And last, but not least, there are the blessed negroes . . ." Booth's voice was drowned out by cries of "Hallelujah!" and "Hosanna!" as a black man in the hall was made to stand up and take a bow, his face breaking into a broad smile.

Then it was Railton's turn to speak. "Why, you may ask, have I chosen seven lasses to go with me? I want to show what women, inspired by the Holy Ghost, can do. It is their task, with me, to gain a firm foothold upon the American continent, then to hand the work over to American officers, for that must be the way to establish the work in that great country. Whether these young women stay or return to their homeland is in the hand of God. But for the present," he raised a clenched fist, "we are going to fight, and we will be victorious."

The following Saturday morning, the soldiers assembled by the hundreds at the Whitechapel Headquarters to escort the invading party of eight to the Tilbury Docks. The day was cloudy and rain threatened, but the spirits of the troops were high, as Railton and Bramwell organized the crowd into some kind of order for the march to Fenchurch Street railway station.

Order established, the procession moved off with Railton at its head, his face beaming. Three of the young women soldiers marched with the Commissioner (Railton had just become the first to be appointed to this rank in the Salvation Army), one carrying the flag of the First Pennsylvania Corps. Next came the remainder of the invasion force with Captain Emma Westbrook carrying the colors of the First New York Corps. They were followed by various officers, including Bramwell, Ballington Booth, and James Dowdle (his violin adding to the merriment of the occasion), the standards of the First Whitechapel and Second Bethnal Green corps, and then a large company of soldiers in a variety of uniforms or street clothes. Finally came Catherine Booth, walking with her younger daughters and a whole host of children enjoying the fun.

As they marched they sang, taking their lead from the irrepressible Dowdle. An enormous crowd of spectators, attracted by the noise and activity, lined the streets of the route to the station. The whole area seemed to grind to a halt, as horse-drawn buses and other vehicles stopped so that their passengers could witness the spectacle.

From Fenchurch Street station they traveled by train to the Tilbury Docks, where the *Australia* awaited her eight excited passengers.

"America for Jesus!" someone shouted from the quay as the invading party embarked. Others echoed the call, and Railton waved his hand and shouted, "Amen!"

Catherine Booth's tears were running down her cheeks, mixing with the rain that had started to fall. Saying "goodbye" to the likeable George Railton was harder even than she had expected.

Bramwell fussed over her. "Mother, you will catch cold."

"I know," she said, "but I can't help it."

"Let me take you to a sheltered spot," her son suggested.

"No, Bramwell, not until the ship has departed," she stubbornly insisted. At 3:40 P.M. the *Australia* moved off. Shouts of "God bless you!" and "The Lord go with you!" rang out over the sea as handkerchiefs and hats waved wildly in the air.

"Till we meet again, George Railton," whispered Catherine.

"What was that, mother?" asked Bramwell.

"Just a prayer, Bramwell. Just a prayer."

17

Skirmishes in New York

*T*he sea voyage was more difficult than expected. Instead of taking the normal ten days, it lasted for twenty-five. The cold, wet weather continued, and as the vessel left the English Channel and launched out into the Atlantic it worsened. Gale force winds made the seas mountainous.

Railton was his normal cheery self. His female companions were the color of the tossing seas—gray-green. Their boldness at their departure from Tilbury had degenerated into the misery of seasickness.

George Railton tried to cheer his troops and began to sing with the howling of the wind and the sound of the engines as his accompaniment. "Oh, we're going to wear a crown . . ." he began. But the women would not be, could not be, comforted. As one vomited into a bucket, the determined leader tried another tack. "Let's conduct a service. There are many men and women on this ship who need saving, and it will take your minds off your problem."

The ship descended into the trough of a wave, and the seven women groaned in unison. "Go away," one grumbled in a faint voice.

"It will take your minds off it, I tell you," he persisted.

The ship rose and dropped again, leaving the "Hallelujah Lasses" with no thoughts of praise. Again they groaned.

Gradually it dawned on Railton that his cheeriness and his attempts to make his colleagues think of matters other than the queasiness of their own stomachs were not helping. As he pondered his next step, one of the now familiar background noises

65

suddenly lessened and then, after a few minutes, stopped altogether. The wind still howled but the engines were silent. Though the Commissioner did not know it, one of the two engines had ruptured and the other shut down while repairs commenced.

The little Salvationist left his companions and ventured out on deck to find out what the problem was. He hung on grimly and inched his way along as the ship tossed and the sea splashed over the decks.

Suddenly the *Australia* lurched more violently than it had before, and the evangelist lost his hold. He fell—slid rapidly to the side of the ship, arms and legs swinging wildly, and almost went over the edge. But at the last minute he grabbed hold of the ship's rails and managed to save himself.

As he recovered from his mishap, discretion became the better part of valor and he slowly, shakily worked his way back to safety and rejoined his sisters below decks.

The engineers were unable to repair the faulty engine, and the ship, now well off course, had to continue the journey with the one that remained. Two days later, as the ship went slowly westward in much calmer seas, Railton organized the fittest of his soldiers to conduct a service up on deck. The two Salvation Army flags, with their *Blood and Fire* emblem and the Stars and Stripes in one corner, fluttered in the brisk breeze. The ship still rolled, but much more gently.

The *Australia* continued her painfully slow progress. Rations were reduced and the passengers were in a mood of depression, apart from the ever-ebullient George Railton. His seven associates also showed improved spirits as the vessel moved through calmer seas, but seasickness was a constant companion of the group. Ship-board services continued, and one woman responded to the Gospel message.

On Thursday, March 4, the *Elysia* rendezvoused with the *Australia* and took on board some of her passengers. Railton refused to leave. "This ship is being prayed for," he reasoned. "Even if it is slow, and even if we might be put on biscuits only, I and my companions will not leave it," he told the ship's captain. The women followed their officer's lead, but kept their doubts about the wisdom of his decision to themselves.

With the reduction in the number of passengers the food rationing tightened no further, and the *Australia* finally docked on

Wednesday March, 10. They looked out over New York, and thanked God for their safe arrival.

With considerable relief the little army disembarked at Old Castle Garden, and fell on their knees on American soil to claim that great land for Jesus.

They set up headquarters at Pickwick Lodging House in Liberty Street, but had great difficulty in finding a suitable meeting place. They met a Mrs. Doolittle, who ran a mission in Baxter Street in a large house that had previously been used as a brothel. She kindly agreed to them using her premises until they could find something of their own.

On Friday, an unexpected visitor arrived at Liberty Street. Emma Morris opened the door and came face-to-face with a strongly built American dressed in a loud check three-piece suit and smoking the biggest cigar she had ever seen.

"I'm Harry Hill," he introduced himself. "I want to see George Railton. I have a proposition for him."

Emma looked at the visitor and wondered what that proposition might be. "You'd better come in," she invited.

She showed Hill into the room that they were using as an office, and introduced him to Railton.

"Pleased to meet you, Mr. Railton," said the American as he moved forward to shake hands. Ash fell from the cigar, held in his other hand. "My name is Harry Hill. I own Hill's Variety Theater."

"I see," said Railton. "What can I do for you?" he asked, half-suspecting the answer.

"Well, I'm looking for a turn on Sunday evening—someone's let me down you see—and I understand from some friends from England that the Salvation Army knows how to attract a good crowd."

George Railton looked at the theater owner. "I don't think you understand, Mr. Hill. We are a religious group. We are here to tell people about the Lord Jesus. We are not entertainers."

"Maybe, maybe, George, but they tell me you do it with a lot of flair, musical instruments, and the like. Great entertainment!"

"Yes, that's true, but—"

Harry Hill cut in, "I know—you are afraid we might not pay enough. Don't worry about that. We pay the best rates."

"It's not that, Mr. Hill. You see, we don't want any money. We'll do it for nothing."

Hill's mouth gaped open, and the hand holding the cigar dropped to his side. More ash fell on the floor. "You don't want money? Well, I guess we'd probably pay you anyway." He thought for a moment. "You don't like playing in theaters, do you?" he guessed.

"Well, not exactly, Mr Hill! In England we often play . . . hold meetings in theaters, but under our own control, not as an act in a show," explained Railton.

"Well, I reckon you're worth taking a chance on, George, and I hope you feel the same way about me. I tell you what. Here's my card. Think about it, and get back to me early this afternoon. No later, mind, as we'll have to advertise."

The Salvationist took the card. "Thank you, Mr. Hill. I will think about it and let you know, one way or the other, by noon."

"Nice meeting you, George. See you later, then." He turned, knocked more ash on the floor and walked out.

Emma Morris, who had not left the room, was standing with hands on hips. "He thinks we're just a music hall act, Commissioner. We can't go just to perform, can we?" She spoke with obvious disgust.

"No, Emma, we can't. But that doesn't mean we can't go and present the Gospel. I'll go and see Mrs. Doolittle and get a third opinion." He hurried round to the missioner and outlined the problem.

"Yes, that sounds like Harry Hill," she said. "Mr. Railton, it's a bad place. Go there and you'll lose your reputation."

Railton smiled. "Mrs. Doolittle, I think you have given me the answer. We have no reputation to lose. We will 'play' for Mr. Hill." He pulled the visitor's card from his pocket and looked at it. "Could you direct me to the corner of Houston and Crosby Streets? I will go to see him right away."

"I'm not sure you are doing the right thing, Mr. Railton, but it's your business, I guess," she said with a shrug of the shoulders. "Come to the door, and I will show you how to get there."

The Salvationist returned the theater man's visit, and they made the arrangements. By the evening, posters advertising the event were scattered around the city.

SALVATION ARMY WILL ATTACK
KINGDOM OF THE DEVIL
HARRY HILL'S VARIETY THEATER
ON SUNDAY MARCH 14, 1880
AT 6:30 P.M.

AFTER WHICH A PANORAMA OF *UNCLE TOM'S
CABIN*

ADMISSION 25¢

They also decided to hold a meeting on Sunday morning in the Baxter Street Mission. Before it was due to start they divided into two groups, one on either side of the road, and slowly worked their way up Greenwich Street. It was foggy and colder than they were used to. They were glad for the warmth of their uniforms.

They spoke to those they encountered and entered saloons to try to entice some of the drinkers to join them at the mission hall. The tavern owners did not take kindly to "religious cranks" trying to take their customers, and had the Salvationists removed. One saloon owner, a German woman, when faced with the offer of salvation at the bar's door, cried out to her husband, "Salvation? Oh, no! Hans, lock the door!" and beat a hasty retreat.

But the time spent scouring the streets had been worthwhile, and a collection of human flotsam, similar to that at Salvation Army meetings in England, had gathered.

The meeting was rowdy and full of interruptions, but at the end several came forward in repentance and were counseled by the young Salvationists.

Elizabeth Pearson was having difficulty with the man she was counseling, so she sought Railton's help. "Commissioner, I can't get anywhere with that man over there," she said pointing him out. "He is very drunk."

Mrs. Doolittle had heard her comments and said, "Very drunk? That's Jimmy Kemp—'Ash Barrel Jimmy.' You ought to see him when he's really drunk!"

"You know him then?" asked Railton.

"Everybody 'round here knows him. He's the worst drunk in New York."

"Really! Why's he called 'Ash Barrel'?"

"The story goes that once he was so drunk, really drunk, that he fell head-first into an ash barrel and got stuck. It was two hours before they were able to get him out. Ever since then he's been known as Ash Barrel Jimmy."

George Railton looked at Jimmy, lounging in a chair, and then at Elizabeth Pearson. "Leave him to me, Elizabeth. Would you get me some coffee, Mrs. Doolittle? Black! Really drunk or not, we are going to have to sober him up." So saying, he walked toward the man, sat beside him, and began to talk to him.

The square-jawed "Ash Barrel Jimmy" was scarcely aware of the Commissioner's words, but Railton persisted. Mrs. Doolittle came with the cup of coffee, and they helped him drink it. Later, Railton tried a more dramatic measure. He threw a bucket of water over him.

Gradually, he became more conscious of his surroundings and Railton's words, but he said little that was coherent. It came almost as a surprise to Railton, when he suddenly said, "But not someone as bad as me. I'm too far gone."

"No one is too far gone. The Lord can save anyone."

Jimmy began to cry. "You mean He can save me?"

"Yes," said Railton, "the Bible says that 'whosoever shall call on the name of Lord shall be saved.' It doesn't say you have to be good, or just not too bad. It says 'whosoever.' That means anybody. That means you."

The drunk sat there still sobbing. Suddenly, with a loud shout he cried out, "O Lord, save me!" and fell on the floor in a faint.

Railton bent over him, took off his own coat and put it under the man's head. Kemp lay there without moving for over ten minutes. He got up a new man.

By early evening news of Ash Barrel Jimmy's conversion was widespread. Well before 6:30 Harry Hill's Variety Theater was packed. The galleries and the pit were filled with a noisy, expectant audience. The theater's walls were lined with vulgar posters, making it seem an odd place for Christian worship. But Railton was prepared to suffer that for the opportunity of preaching to a full house.

He did preach, too, but strangely lacked his usual fire, and the audience, expecting entertainment, were very restless. After two hours of the ministries of Railton and his associates and no apparent results, the *Uncle Tom's Cabin* panorama took over.

The next day they received word from the mayor that they were forbidden to preach or evangelize in the streets. The Commissioner was angry and penned a reply:

To his Honor the Mayor of the city of New York, I, G. S. Railton, by the grace of God and by the appointment of William Booth, General of the Salvation Army, Commissioner for the various States and countries of North, and South America, send greeting.

Whereas, under the authority granted to me I have appointed certain officers to carry on within this city such operations as may be necessary to cause those who are at present in rebellion against God to submit to Him, that they may be saved.

And whereas it is an essential part of such operations that the people who habitually avoid entering places of worship should be followed in the public thoroughfares and should by means of services held there be made willing to attend meetings indoors. Whereas you, the Mayor of this city, refuse to grant permission to me to speak in the public thoroughfares.

Now, therefore, I hereby most respectfully request in the name of the Lord God of Hosts that before six P.M. on Thursday, March 18, 1880, an engagement be delivered to me at the above address from the government of this city to permit any person acting under my direction to proclaim salvation in the streets.

I hereby further give you notice that failing the delivery of such engagement before the above time I shall remove the Headquarters of this Army in America to some city where equal privileges are enjoyed by all citizens, ordained or not.

18

Railton in St. Louis

*B*efore the deadline Railton received a communication from the mayor that such permission would not be granted, so at the end of the week he and five of his colleagues went to Philadelphia to join the Shirleys and establish their headquarters there. Emma Westbrook and Mary Coleman were left in charge of the New York corps.

When the group arrived in Philadelphia the Commissioner appointed the three Shirleys to the rank of captain. Soon after the newcomers' arrival a reporter from *The Philadelphia Times* went to interview the leaders of this strange new church.

The reporter asked his questions. The Shirleys and the recently arrived additions answered politely and willingly. The journalist scribbled the answers in his notebook. As the interview ended the man thanked the Salvationists for the story and prepared to leave.

"Now, my brother, how is it with you? Have you given your heart to God?" asked Anna Shirley, her round face beaming.

The reporter stopped, blushed and mumbled his reply. "I came here to interview you, not be interviewed."

"Young man, you must repent. 'The Kingdom of Heaven is at hand,' " Anna exhorted. "We will pray over you."

"I'm afraid it won't do any good," said the embarrassed writer.

"Well, it certainly won't do any harm," responded Mrs. Shirley determinedly. She placed her hands on his shoulders, and forced him to his knees beside the parlor table. She then knelt beside him. Eliza Shirley quickly removed the cups from the table, and Rachel and Elizabeth replaced them with hymnbooks.

Eliza flicked through one of the books and found a suitable song, which she sang. The other Salvationists joined in as they found the right page, kneeling in a circle around their visitor:

Hallelujah, it is done,
I believe in the Son,
I'm saved by the blood
Of the Crucified One.

As the singing ended Anna prayed loudly and earnestly for the conversion of the reporter. More hymns followed and more prayers.

As the Salvationists fervently pleaded for his soul the bewildered young man slowly rose to his feet, stammering, "L-look— I'm really sorry, b-but I must be going. My editor needs this report. I'm s-sorry." He hastily left the house in spite of the protests of the persistent Anna Shirley.

The work in America grew rapidly. Two months after the arrival of the Railton-led invasion force there were nearly 500 soldiers, including sixteen officers. A station had been established in Newark as well as in New York and Philadelphia. One disappointment the Commissioner expressed was that there were very few black people joining the movement. They were attending the meetings, but few were being converted, and even fewer joined the ranks.

As summer came around, the group of English missionaries found the heat trying. All of the women were sick at some time, Emma Morris frequently. Even Railton's normally robust health was below par.

This confirmed to the Commissioner the wisdom of his original plan, to hand the work over to American officers, and let his seven companions return to England as soon as the work had taken root. All of those women, with the exception of Emma Westbrook, returned to their homeland within two years of their arrival. Railton was to do likewise, but by then the work had such an impetus that the devil himself could not halt it.

Season succeeded season, and Railton's vision grew with each. Winter found him as far inland as St. Louis. His reputation had preceded him, for he toured the various public meeting places in the city trying to rent one for his crusades, but to no avail. The owners were afraid that the kind of people this man was supposed to attract would wreck their buildings.

Railton was not easily beaten. He was an innovator. He decided to hold his meetings on the frozen Mississippi River, which required neither rental nor permit.

So one Sunday he and two of his faithful English helpers began to give out leaflets for the meeting later that day. When they walked onto the ice, their congregation, many of whom were already happily skating on the thick ice, gathered around. They began the service by singing a hymn. Some of the skaters joined in. Many of their usual congregation were continually on the move, but it did not deter the dedicated Railton. His feet, which were wrapped in newspaper and string because he could not afford shoes, were frozen, but he preached with fire. Yet no converts were made that day at their ice-bound meeting place.

The going was much tougher in St. Louis than it had been on the East Coast. Reduced to virtual destitution, Railton sent the girls back to Philadelphia, and continued the work on his own. It was two months before there was any significant impact. In those two months he ate only rarely and slept on a pile of *War Crys*.

On January 1, 1881, Railton received a telegram. It was a command from his General to return to England. Obedient soldier though he was, he believed he should remain in America for a while longer, so he wrote to Booth requesting to stay.

Back came Booth's cable: "Must have you here."

Again, Railton replied requesting to stay longer, afraid that the base he had worked so hard to build was not a solid enough foundation for a successful ministry.

But the General had problems too. The Army was rapidly expanding in Britain and overseas, persecution was rampant, and Booth firmly believed he needed his one and only Commissioner by his side.

Booth's third telegram read: "Come alone."

Railton argued no longer, and set out on his journey back to England. While crossing the Mississippi he wrote a hymn, which is an excellent testimony to the dedication of George Scott Railton:

> No home on earth have I,
> No nation owns my soul;
> My dwelling-place is the Most High,
> I'm under His control:
> O'er all the earth alike,

My Father's grand domain,
Each land and sea with Him I liked;
O'er all He yet shall reign.
With Thee, my God, is home;
With Thee is endless joy;
With Thee in ceaseless rest I roam,
With Thee, can death destroy?
With Thee, the east, the west,
The north, the south, are one;
The battle's front I love the best,
And yet—"Thy will be done!"

19

Assault on Australia

*I*n Australia each of the six states has its own character, summed up *by* the questions the inhabitants ask their visitors. In Western Australia, where most ships visiting Australia make their first call, they ask, "Where do you come from?" In Victoria in the southeast, the country's main academic state, the question is, "What school did you go to?" New South Welshmen, whose capital, Sydney, is the business center of Australia, ask, "What do you do for a living?" In the cool but friendly southern island, Tasmania, the question is, "What would you like to eat?" And in Queensland, the gigantic, rough-and-ready, northeastern state, one hears, "What'll you have to drink, mate?"

It is perhaps surprising that the work of the Australian Salvation Army started in Adelaide, the South Australian capital. The question there is, "What church do you go to?" for Adelaide is noted for its beautiful churches and cathedrals.

At the time of the Army's attack on Australia it was not a country as such, rather a collection of colonies administered from Britain. John Gore had been converted through the ministry of William Booth in 1868 and had joined the Christian Mission, becoming known as the "Happy Milkman." Gore and his wife Sarah emigrated to Australia and he became a ganger on the South Australian railways.

Edward Saunders had been brought up in Bradford, and had come to know the Lord through James Dowdle and, like Gore, attached himself to the Christian Mission. He too migrated to Adelaide, where his wife died, leaving him to care for his three children.

Gore and Saunders met at an evangelistic meeting in Adelaide in 1880, and were thrilled to discover that they both had connections with what was by then the Salvation Army. Adelaide may well have been the city of churches, but Gore and Saunders knew that much of its population was untouched by the Gospel. They came to the firm conviction that their new home needed the Salvation Army.

They began by asking around to see if others would be interested in establishing the organization there. They found among the recent migrants several with Army associations.

John Gore wrote to William Booth, telling him of their desire to launch the Salvation Army in the Antipodes. He closed: "Come over and help us. The Salvation Army is what we want. The churches are asleep here, and a good waking up would do us good." Saunders wrote offering to pay the fare of workers. Both letters were published in the *War Cry* and Booth suggested that his people make the request a matter for prayer. "We must go'" he wrote. "It is only a question of time."

The General did not view with any enthusiasm the prospect of key workers traveling to the other side of the world, while Railton was still in America and persecution was increasing throughout Britain. Someone had to go—but who?

Bramwell, the recently appointed Chief of Staff (the rank immediately below General in the Salvation Army hierarchy) replied to Gore and Saunders, advising them that the matter was under consideration, and that they hoped to send officers to them soon. The reply was received with great enthusiasm and Gore, Saunders, and their supporters decided to hold meetings under the Salvation Army name without further delay.

Sunday, September 5, 1880, saw the first two Salvation Army services on Australian soil. The first, typically, was in the open air. That afternoon the handful of Salvationists met in Adelaide Botanic Park, and proclaimed the Gospel under a large gum tree. Saunders accompanied the singing on an old harmonium and John Gore preached from the back of a greengrocer's cart. That evening the second meeting was held in the Labor League Hall, and five people were converted.

A few weeks later, Gore wrote to the General again:

"The Salvation Army has commenced in this sunny land," he triumphantly informed Booth. "We need you as quick as fire and steam can bring you. The Lord is doing a great work here. The Army is led by me until some of you arrive. Since we commenced the Lord has blessed us in every way, but we have it real hot from the enemy of souls."

At the English headquarters it was obvious that there could be no further delay, and "Glory" Tom Sutherland and his appropriately-named wife Adelaide were chosen to go. Before her marriage she was Adelaide Milner, and was nicknamed "Hot" Milner because of her fiery evangelical enthusiasm. The innocent expression on her heart-shaped face hid her fervent temperament. She did not stop short of dragging hesitant would-be converts to their knees. The General once told her, "Adelaide, you will find that if you mix a little sugar with your pills, they'll go down better." She did sweeten her methods, but she did not compromise her message.

The Sutherlands were greeted in Adelaide by sixty-eight Salvationists and sympathizers. Tom and Adelaide Sutherland disembarked, wearing the first full Salvation Army uniforms seen in Australasia. They carried with them an additional twelve uniforms, for whoever of the Australian contingent they would fit.

By mid-April they had erected their own hall in the less glamorous part of the town, established a brass band (one of the Army's first), and were rapidly growing in number.

Work began soon in Sydney and Melbourne, and later in Brisbane where it was more difficult to establish a base.

20

Melbourne and Brisbane

While Major James Barker was in command of the Australian work, he and Captain John Horsley spoke to a man at the Salvation Army office in Melbourne. The man looked older than his sixty years, and had a desperate, almost wild, appearance. His hair was dishevelled and his clothes, though clean, were strangely ill-fitting and his face bore a distinctly hunted look.

"What's your name?" asked Barker.

The man's hands moved restlessly in his lap and it seemed ages before he answered the question. Finally he said, "John Taylor, sir."

"How can we help you, Mr. Taylor?"

Again, Taylor hesitated before speaking. He looked at the two men, then away again, before fixing his eyes on Barker's. "Give me a chance, Mr. Barker. Give me a chance," he pleaded. "I've spent forty years in prison, and don't have much time left. I don't want to spend me final days there. Give me a chance, please, Mr. Barker."

"Do you have any family?" questioned Horsley.

"No, I ain't got none. Me wife left me years ago, and I don't blame her for that. I've got no one. You see, Mr. Barker, I need a 'ome. I've never really 'ad a 'ome. When you come out of prison the thing you need most is a 'ome. That's why so many keep going back, 'cause they've got nowhere else to go," explained John Taylor.

The message was clear to Barker and Horsley, but they were unsure what action to take. They sat and thought for a moment,

79

then Barker said, "If you will just wait outside the office for a minute, Mr. Taylor, we will see what we can do for you." The three men rose and Taylor was shown out of the room. "What can we do, John?" asked Barker.

Horsley was lost in thought. "What did you say? Oh, yes. Well, we have to do something. The poor bloke looks as though he doesn't have much longer to go anyway," he observed.

"As he said, the first thing is a roof over his head, then a job, I suppose," said the Major.

"I've been thinking, Major. What if I take him into my home for a few days to see if he really means to go straight. Then we can try to find him a permanent place and a job," Horsley offered.

"And what if he doesn't?"

"Well, we can cross that bridge when, and if, we come to it," said the brave Horsley.

"All right," said Barker. "He's yours. Take care, and let me know how things go."

Horsley smiled, "Thank you . . . I think." He left the office and took John Taylor home with him. Within a week Taylor had proved himself and the Salvationist had found him both a job and accommodation in Bendigo.

For twelve months Taylor's words haunted Barker: "When you come out of prison the thing you need most is a 'ome." Then, relieved of the national command, Barker had time to devote to finding homes for ex-prisoners.

First he found a suitable house in Melbourne. He then picked his man to meet the prisoners as they were released, Captain Bill Shepherd. Shepherd, no stranger to the inside of prison himself, was the ideal man. He knew what it was like to be incarcerated and then thrown out to a hostile world, where the opportunity to "go straight" was rarely given.

Barker organized the home and Shepherd quickly filled it. Soon it was working effectively. The ex-prisoners were allowed to stay until they had found work. Help was also given by the Salvationists in finding suitable employment.

This "Prison Gate Home" was the first to be established by the Salvation Army anywhere in the world. Six years later, with this as its prototype, such projects became an integral part of the Army's social work.

Brisbane, Queensland's capital, proved much harder to penetrate with the Gospel.

Shortly after Gore and Saunders commenced Army activity in Adelaide, a Mr. and Mrs. Albert McNaught began holding street meetings in Brisbane, and later hired a hall in Charlotte Street. They requested that officers be sent from England, but none came and the work slowly came to an end.

Two more unsuccessful attempts were made in 1883. It was not until 1885, when Adjutant and Mrs. Edward Wright, Staff Officer Reuben Edwards and Captain Thomas Bowerman were despatched from Melbourne, that the work finally gained a firm footing in Queensland.

The new arrivals were shown the old building in Charlotte Street used by their predecessors. Outside was the sign "THE SALVATION ARMY." They added the grafitto "UNDER NEW MANAGEMENT" and launched their attack.

They held their open-air meetings in George Street, and then marched round into Charlotte to their stark barracks. The hall had a corrugated iron roof. In summer it was intolerably hot, and earned the nickname "Nebuchadnezzar's Furnace." When it rained the drumming on the roof almost drowned out the considerable noise of their meetings, and the water found the many holes in the roof and dripped upon saint and sinner alike.

As with all new Salvation Army ventures, the First Brisbane Corps suffered persecution. The open-airs, led by Edward Wright on his cornet, were often disrupted by stone-throwing mobs, who followed them on their march back to the hall. Wright was also jailed for 48 hours for playing his instrument in the street, and a petition was organized to protest about the outrageous activities of this strange sect.

Support was also forthcoming. When Wright was considering selling his cornet (with hindsight unthinkable for a Salvationist) to buy the necessities of life for his destitute group, a local business man donated £10 and promised to repeat it monthly.

This time the organization was firmly established in Brisbane, and from there gradually spread throughout Queensland.

21

Operation France

*T*he launching of the Army's work in America and Australia had not been planned. Their next missionary enterprise was. There had been voices raised from inside and outside the organization about attacking Europe, and France was the country most commonly mentioned. Katie Booth also just happened to be learning French.

For centuries there had been antipathy between the French and the English, and though there had not been a war between them since the defeat of Napoleon Bonaparte over sixty years before, a state of mutual suspicion and dislike still existed.

The Victorian British saw the French as decadent and thus inferior to themselves. Sarah Mumford had even forbidden her daughter Catherine to learn French, that she might not be corrupted by the works of such authors as Voltaire. Catherine had always regretted not being given the opportunity to learn the language, not that she had any sympathies with Voltaire's philosophy and the writings of many other French authors. But she believed she was quite able to decide for herself which French writers were suitable for her to read. So Catherine encouraged her eldest daughter to learn the language which had been closed to her.

In February 1881 William Booth announced in the *War Cry* that his Army was to invade France. The leader of the expeditionary force was to be his twenty-two-year-old daughter, Katie, who was still engrossed in her language studies.

Countess Cairns was shocked. She was not alone. How could the Booths possibly consider sending a young Christian Englishwoman—especially their own daughter—to a country like France? Catherine Booth consoled the worried Countess, telling her that the Lord would protect the fair-haired Katie.

Katie was nobody's fool. She had been preaching since she was thirteen, and the kind of audiences she usually preached to were often little more than mobs. The family nicknamed her "Blucher" after the General who served with Wellington. Few people got the better of her.

Katie was accompanied by two nineteen-year-old lieutenants, Adelaide Cox and Florence Soper. Adelaide's father was a Church of England vicar who had strong sympathies with the Salvation Army. Florence's father, a doctor, was appalled at the news of her impending crusade to France.

The three young women began the work of *Armee du Salut* in Paris, in a hall that could hold six hundred people. None of them had a fluent command of the language. Florence was probably the most proficient. But all three had a dedication to their cause, and a sincere belief in God's call to them to France.

Their initial efforts were unsuccessful. They wandered around the Parisian cafes, singing and praying in the best French they could manage. The locals laughed. The French always suspected that the English were peculiar, now here on their doorstep was confirmation.

Over several weeks the mood of their mission field changed from the gently mocking to the openly antagonistic. One trick employed by the less gallant Frenchmen was to approach the Salvationists from behind, grab the strings of their bonnets and pull until the girls choked.

But gradually dedication, persistence, and prayer won the day. The numbers attending the meetings increased. French men and women were converted, which became a great aid when trying to communicate the Gospel.

Opposition continued—indeed increased—and on several instances the police forbade them to conduct street meetings because of the unruly behavior of the crowds they attracted. Some of the French believed that they were Jesuits, and the Salvationists received the hatred that many of the people had at that time for that Catholic order.

In April *La Marechale* (Katie's new nickname, meaning the

Marshal) became ill through overwork, and the eighteen-year-old Herbert Booth was promptly dispatched to lead the advance into French territory until she had recovered. Herbert, like James Dowdle, was highly skilled on the violin, and he put a new dimension upon their meetings. Herbert was slim—even scrawny—and shorter than the other members of the Booth household. But like all the Booths, he was zealous for his God.

The congregations continued to grow, and a larger hall was hired on the Quai du Valmy. It was capable of holding over a thousand people. Herbert led the singing with his vigorous Dowdle-inspired style of playing, while Florence, Adelaide, and La Marechale preached to the Parisians. When Katie had almost fully recovered Herbert handed back the French command to his sister.

Countess Cairns' concerns about sending three maiden ladies into what she thought of as decadent France were not entirely without justification. One Frenchman accosted Katie while she was preaching around the cafes. La Marechale was rarely at a loss for words, but on this occasion she was dumbfounded. The would-be paramour, taking her silence for approval, asked where they might meet. Katie, fully recovered from the shock of the man's suggestion, looked him in the eye, breathed in deeply, and said resolutely, "Before the Throne of God."

The man, even more shocked by that thought than Katie had been by his, stood for a moment stunned, then turned, and ran from the scene. The other people in the cafe who had heard the exchange burst into laughter at the unexpected outcome. One of them was a newspaper reporter, who made the most of the story in the next day's editions.

The growing Armee du Salut had reached the stage where they needed a French equivalent of the *War Cry*. They had no shortage of material to put in it. They had a printer willing to undertake the work for them, but what should they call it? It was at this point that their limited French almost spelled disaster. Katie was quite set on the title *Amour,* which she saw as an expression of God's love for mankind, and their loving concern for the French race. Her two compatriots liked the title. The French soldiers were horrified. The thought of walking the streets of Paris shouting "*Amour,* un sou!" was too terrible to contemplate. The locals carefully explained to their commander the difficulty, and after a lengthy, embarrassed silence, La Marechale agreed to name the paper *En Avant.*

A second corps was begun in November 1882 in rue Oberkampf, and Catherine Booth went to Paris to celebrate the occasion. To advertize the first services Florence and Adelaide paraded up and down the nearby streets with sandwich-boards. Pushed and jostled, they persisted in their attempts to publicize the new hall. Laughter and scorn did not daunt them—they were serving Jesus, and that was all that mattered.

By the time the first service was due to start, the hall was packed with an unruly crowd. Many were shouting, swearing, and drinking from bottles of wine. When Katie stood on the platform and tried to call the gathering to order, she was totally unsuccessful. The noise and boisterous behavior continued. La Marechale looked questioningly at her mother.

"Let's go into the thick of them, Katie," said Catherine.

So mother and daughter left the platform, went down to the center of the hall and Katie climbed up on one of the benches.

"Men and women of Paris," she called in a loud voice, "we bring you the good news of the Lord Jesus Christ."

"We don't want your Jesus," snarled a man close by.

"But Jesus wants you," she persisted.

"We will not listen to you," came another shout. "Down with the Jesuits!"

"But we are not Jesuits," said La Marechale.

"Vive la liberte!" called another. His words were echoed by some of his companions.

"Amen!" shouted Katie, glad to have something to agree with.

"We will have liberty, but no 'Amens,' " came the response.

"We don't want your Jesus," repeated the first man, and rushing forward pushed over the courageous Salvationist.

As she hit the floor the hall erupted in loud laughter. Her assailant leaned over the bench and spat on her. "Keep your religion," he said venomously.

To one side of the hall a group had pushed some of the wooden benches up against the wall. In the cleared space they began to dance the can-can. Men and women with linked arms wildly kicked their legs and sang loudly.

Catherine helped her daughter up.

"I think we had all better leave, Madame Booth," came the gentle voice of Captain Edouard Becquet from behind them.

"We can't leave," said Katie. "Not while there are souls to save."

"I think Captain Becquet is right, my dear," said her mother. "We can do nothing here now, and the situation is dangerous."

"But we Booths are born to danger," protested her daughter.

Katie was strong-willed, but her mother was even more so. "Katie, we have no time to argue," insisted the older woman. Then, turning to Becquet, "Captain, make sure all our people get out safely. We will look after ourselves." Catherine took a tight grip on her daughter's arm, and hurried her to the front door. As they approached it two big men moved to block it. The two women stopped.

"Step aside, messieurs," instructed Catherine.

The two men neither moved nor spoke.

"We wish to pass," she said forcefully.

One of the men lowered his hand and slowly drew a long knife from its sheath. He held it threateningly toward the Salvationists.

"Excuse us, messieurs—we must go," said Catherine, and still holding Katie's arm, marched swiftly forward and slipped between their two adversaries as they parted in astonishment. Meanwhile, Becquet succeeded in getting all the other Salvationists away through a back door.

The next day they returned to the hall to clean up the expected mess. The sight that met their eyes was even worse than they had anticipated. All of the benches were either tipped over or wrecked, most of the windows had been smashed, and glass littered the floor. Obscene graffiti decorated the walls, and spittle and vomit spattered the floor. The hall was unrecognizable as the one they had proudly set up less then twenty-four hours before.

Devotedly they began to repair the damage and get the hall ready for the next meeting. Salvationists at times retreated, but they never gave up.

22

Railton Returns

William Booth sat at his desk at the Army's Whitechapel headquarters on April 11, 1881. He and his eldest son were sifting through the recently delivered correspondence piled on his desk. They had news of the jailing and speedy release of the Shirleys in Philadelphia, word of success from the Sutherlands in Adelaide, reports of persecution in various towns throughout Britain, and tales of dissent in the ranks.

"Nothing from Railton!" grumbled the General. His stomach was troubling him and upsetting his mood. "Where is he, Bramwell?" He thumped his fist on the table in frustration. "He should be back by now." Booth took the letters in his hands and dropped them back on the desk. "We need him to help us sort this lot out, now. Where is he?"

"He'll be back soon, General. Railton is not one to disobey an order, or shirk his duty. I am sure he will arrive soon."

"But why hasn't he kept in touch?" The General was interrupted by a rap on the door, and a creaking as it opened.

"You called for me, General," said the little figure standing in the doorway. Railton was grinning from ear to ear.

"Railton!" exclaimed Booth, his mood dramatically changing. "Brother Railton, we are so glad to see you!"

Bramwell rushed at his spiritual brother and flung his arms around him. "It is so good to see you, George. So good to have you back. How are you?"

"Fit and well really, Bramwell. Nothing to be concerned about, praise God!" replied the Commissioner. But in reality the rigors of his campaign in America had left him anything but fit and well.

87

"Railton, our little Army is bursting the world," said the General, standing to greet his subordinate. "It's spreading rapidly throughout our land. We have a foothold in Australia and France, as well as your achievements in America. Railton, God is making us march at a pretty fast pace. I need you for a hundred and one things."

"General, I believe I should go back to St. Louis. There is so much to be done there," stated Railton firmly.

"Yes, Railton, I know! I know the work there needs you, but we need you more here. The fact is, I can no longer spare you for any length of time in one place. We have trouble in Luton. John Mobley is sick and a rival faction is disrupting our work. I want you to go there first thing in the morning," ordered the General.

"Yes, General," Railton responded obediently. An order from the General face-to-face was far more commanding than a telegram. "Who is to take over the American command, then?"

"Tom Moore. We have promoted him to Major, and he leaves England next week," replied Booth.

"Are you sure he is the right man for the job?" questioned the Commissioner.

Bramwell broke in. "To be honest, George, we are not sure. He is the best we have available. Our resources are stretched very thinly at the moment. Our supply of experienced officers is very limited. We will just have to pray he will succeed. But you, George, you look all worn out. You had better go and have a rest and prepare for tomorrow. I'll fill you in on the details later."

"Let's have some knee-drill first," said the General.

So saying, he fell to his knees and his colleagues followed his example. The three men earnestly besought God's blessing on their work. Later Railton went to the Booth home to rest, and on the following day went on his rescue mission to the corps in Luton.

In September their headquarters was moved. The site in Whitechapel had been proving less and less satisfactory as the work grew and grew. The new location at 101 Queen Victoria Street in the city of London was appropriately named the International Headquarters. It was situated close enough to the East End of London, still the heart of the work, but was also convenient for most of the main line railway stations, which was essential because of the amount of traveling the leaders now did.

23

Capturing a Stronghold

Up and down the City Road,
In and out the Eagle;
That's the way the money goes,
Pop! goes the weasel.

A small group of children skipped down the City Road, singing the ditty which never failed to rankle Booth. He was in a hansom returning to the International Headquarters, and the cab had slowed as it was passing the complex that housed the Grecian Theater and Eagle Tavern.

The children were living results of the reality behind the rhyme, barefooted and shabbily dressed. Booth peered through the cab's window, looked at the children, and watched the crowds making their way down Shepherdess Walk in the warm spring sunshine to enter the tavern. He guessed that the children's parents would be in The Eagle, drinking and making the "money go." He knew better than most the significance of the verse. "Pop!" meant to pawn, and a "weasel" was a watch. As an ex-pawnbroker's assistant he was painfully aware that the poor frequently pawned their possessions to raise money for drink. It was not a coincidence that a pawnbroker's shop was nearby.

He hated The Eagle. Behind the pleasant facade of wrought-iron gates and attractive gardens, Booth knew it hosted not only drunkenness but also rampant prostitution. If only he could get it closed—but how?

Five years earlier, in 1877, Railton had suggested opening up a center for training personnel adjacent to The Eagle. It seemed to him that there could not be a better spot for training young hopefuls of the Christian Mission than in the heart of the devil's territory. Booth had never forgotten Railton's idea, but no opportunity had arisen to make it a reality, though for some time now work had been going on to convert an unused orphanage in Clapton into a Congress Hall, part of the purpose of which would be to train officers.

The cab continued its journey along City Road and Moorgate, then into Queen Victoria Street. When Booth arrived, Bramwell and Railton gave him the latest details on the preparations for the opening of the Congress Hall. Thoughts of The Eagle were pushed from his mind. The Congress Hall was duly opened a month later amid joyous celebrations.

Shortly afterward Bramwell noisily hurried a tall officer into Booth's office. "General," said Bramwell, "we have some terrific news. Tell him, John."

Booth had looked up immediately as the men barged into the room, and his eyes fixed upon the bearded face of John Lawley.

"The Eagle's up for sale, General. The whole lot—the tavern, theater, dancing pavilion, and billiard rooms. All of it," said the excited man.

Booth's face beamed. "Is it?" he asked, but did not wait for confirmation. "How much? What are they asking?"

Bramwell hesitated. His face showed a moment of doubt.

"£16,750, General, with three months to pay," he answered.

The General's smile disappeared. He sat in silence for a moment, his left hand running through his hair. Suddenly his hand ceased. He looked at his two companions. "We can do it! Praise God, we can do it!" he blurted out.

"But where will the money come from?" asked Lawley. "We've just now finished paying for the Congress Hall. I don't know that our people can afford to give more."

"Have faith, brother Lawley. Do you think God will fail us when we have such an excellent opportunity to smash the devil's stronghold? We will ask our people for more, and anyone else we can think of," encouraged the General enthusiastically. "Bramwell, organize some letters requesting donations. You know who to send them to, our usual benefactors. We had better extend our list, I think. Send one to all of the archbishops, any bishop likely to be sympathetic—politicians too. And businessmen—

don't forget them." Booth spoke rapidly, but Bramwell took it all in.

"How about the Queen?" suggested the Chief-of-Staff.

"Yes, Bramwell! A great idea! Send one to her Majesty, and other members of the Royal Family too. We will get the money. God will not see us short on this. I am sure it is His will. Arrange an appointment with our solicitors at once, too, so we can set the wheels in motion."

The letters outlining the plan and requesting donations began to leave that day. One of the first donations came from the Archbishop of Canterbury, Dr. Tait. Recognition of the Salvation Army from the leading men in the Church of England had increased to such an extent that the Archbishop of York had approached Booth earlier in the year to discuss ways in which the two churches could cooperate to spread the Gospel.

The front page of the *War Cry* of June 29, 1882, told the story:

CONVERSION OF THE EAGLE

Conversion of The Eagle Tavern, The Grecian Theater, Dancing Pavilion and Ground, Dancing Saloon and Assembly Rooms, Capable of Seating in All 10,000 People.

We have secured the lease of all the above notorious premises for £16,750. Converts who have drunk, danced and sinned there repeatedly in the dark days of their former life assure us that the souls of more young people have gone down to destruction through the scenes of revelry which have been witnessed on these premises than from any other popular resort in London.

WE HAVE ONLY THREE WEEKS in which to complete payment, so that we must have help at once.

The Archbishop of Canterbury was almost the first to assist us in the matter. The Bishop of London, the Right Hon. Earl Cairns, the ex-Lord Mayor, and others of influence have also expressed their warm sympathy.

Remember there is but three weeks, and let everybody and every corps that is able, do something at once.

The Archbishop of Canterbury had been happy to contribute, her Majesty was not. Queen Victoria was not amused. She had never forgiven Booth for calling himself General, and for founding an army in England, a land which had one army and one army only—hers. A polite but negative letter came from Sir Henry Ponsonby on her behalf, saying that her Majesty would not be contributing to the fund.

Booth, with a stroke of genius, published the letter on the front page of the *War Cry* on July 13, suggesting that if they did not have the Queen's money (no doubt she was short of ready cash) at least they had her moral support.

Donations, mostly small, began to stream into International Headquarters. They came mainly from corps and individual Salvationists, though a few more people of note did contribute. An "Eagle Sunday" was held when a special offering was taken up for the fund. The *War Cry* faithfully recorded the donations in its July and early August issues.

Possession of the property was finally taken on Saturday, August 12. Railton was placed in charge of the procession intended to celebrate the capture.

As early as 5 A.M. Salvationists began to assemble in Finsbury Square, near the boundary of the city of London. Railton, who had had little more than two hours' sleep the previous night, was busily organizing his forces. Most of the soldiers wore uniforms, but there was still no standardization. Navy blue was the predominant color, and some men wore red jerseys. There was a strange assortment of caps, helmets, berets and bonnets on an even stranger selection of heads. The giant frame of Dr. John Morrison was clearly visible, and William Monk was also present.

Railton was speaking to the leader of the cadets' band, which had been chosen to lead the march. "We'll go straight down the City Road, into Shepherdess Walk, then enter through the main door."

"As you say, Commissioner. I've heard rumors that there will be some trouble, but I can't see it at this hour of the morning," said the bandsman.

"Any hour can be the hour for trouble, Bert, so be ready. The police have been alerted," responded Railton.

At 5:30 Ballington Booth approached George Railton. "I think we're ready, Commissioner," he said. "There's about a thousand of us, I'd say," he added, extending his hand in the direction of the massing troops.

"Right you are, Ballington. I'll go ahead with the band, and you can lead the rest of the soldiers. And Ballington, place Dr.

Morrison and Monk one on either side of the procession, just in case."

"Yes, Commissioner," said Ballington with a smile.

The march began. The band walked out into the road, playing as they went. The color party followed, followed by Ballington and the rest of the gathering.

The band's lively playing attracted attention as they moved north along City Road, and marched past Wesley's Chapel. A sprinkling of people lined the street, watching curiously. Two policemen walked on one side of the road, keeping pace with the bandsmen. After they crossed Old Street, the number of onlookers increased dramatically, and the mood of mild curiosity changed to one of aggression.

" Ands off The Eagle!" came a shout.

"We don't want your army!" rose another.

A stone thrown at the front of the procession missed all the bandsmen, but clanged against a cornet, making its player drop his instrument. He hurriedly bent to retrieve it while his colleagues continued on their way. Those in the crowd who saw it laughed and pointed at the man.

As the crowd had grown, so had the police presence. The crowd's manner was increasingly threatening, but the police kept them at bay.

"Where's that General Booth?" said a voice from the crowd. "We'll lynch 'im if we get 'old of 'im!"

Ballington felt a prickling sensation on the back of his neck. *It is as well they don't know who I am,* he thought.

A dead rat was flung at Railton, who was still proudly marching in front of the band. It hit him on the leg and fell to the ground. He stooped to pick it up. Railton worked on the principle that if one held on to what had been thrown, it could not be thrown again.

"Beer, not Bibles!" came another call from the angry crowd.

"What are we to do for a livin' now!" shouted a woman.

The Salvationists continued their march, flanked by a still increasing but thinly spread contingent of police. Railton found their presence in such numbers and their obvious intention to protect the marchers surprising. He was more used to the police beating a hasty retreat at the sign of trouble and leaving his soldiers to their own fate.

More missiles were thrown—stones, mud, rotten fruit, and dead animals—but the parade continued.

Shortly before six o'clock Railton and the band turned onto Shepherdess Walk, greeted by shouts and screams from the assembled thousands. The police were working hard to keep the crowd back, and numerous offenders were dragged away when they tried to break the police lines.

The Salvation Army flag was already fluttering in the breeze above The Eagle Tavern. As the procession approached, Salvationists within the complex opened the iron gates at the main entrance for their comrades to file in.

Behind the gates were three large wooden doors headed, "Billiards," "Boxes and Stalls" and "Pit." Above the center door was a sign saying that the center would ". . . reopen early in September under Salvation management."

Morrison and Monk stood on guard at the entrance until the thousand Salvationists had entered the grounds; the gates were then closed and locked.

Suddenly one section of the crowd broke through the police cordon and converged on the gates. Some of the police pursued to try to regain their lost advantage. It was only reinforcements arriving on the scene at that moment that prevented a full scale attack on the building. Gradually the police regained control, forcing the aggressors back.

At the conclusion of the service the leaders considered how to get the people away safely. One suggestion was to leave by the stage door and along New North Road, avoiding the mob in front of the building.

"It sounds like a retreat to me," said Railton sternly.

"Perhaps we should look at it more as a strategic withdrawal, Commissioner," countered Ballington. "I believe you will find the new route almost as hot as the old when the crowd gets to know of it."

"Yes, Ballington, you're right. Inform our brothers and sisters, then commend us to the Lord."

The young Booth walked to the front of the platform, held up his hand for silence, and advised his flock of their new direction. Then, falling to his knees, he prayed loudly for divine protection. After the prayer, the large contingent of soldiers, following Railton, began to file through the stage door out into the almost deserted street; Ballington and Morrison remained until the end, making sure that everyone was out.

The band stayed silent until well away from The Grecian but eventually, under the Commissioner's instructions, blasted forth as they reached the New North Road. They then marched along Pitfield Street.

Gradually the mob, informed that their prey was escaping, converged on Pitfield Street from City Road and Old Street. The police, heavily outnumbered, found it increasingly difficult to restrain them.

As they crossed Old Street, the Salvationists found themselves entirely surrounded by thousands of screaming men and women, and only managed to move on because the police were able to clear a path for them. Blows rained on those in the outside ranks, as the attackers wielded sticks and metal bars. Railton had a gash on the right side of his cheek, but still he marched in front of his troops, his arms full of dead rats, sticks, stones, and other missiles.

The parade ended when they marched down Shoreditch High Street and into Liverpool Street Station, to the astonishment of the travelers and railway workers.

Here the Salvationists dispersed, most catching trains to destinations in the East End of London.

During the next five weeks alterations were made to the interior of the buildings to make them suitable for Army purposes. The General visited them frequently and the crowd, which seemed to keep vigil night and day, singled him out for special treatment. Every time he arrived he was set upon by the mob, and had to be repeatedly rescued by the police. On the first two occasions he tried to pacify the crowd from the safe side of the gates, but this only further antagonized it. On later visits he made no such attempts.

The Grecian was reopened under the Salvation Army flag on Thursday, September 21. The theater was packed with the faithful, and people were also seated in what had been the main dance hall, the doors adjoining the two areas, wide open.

Both the General and his wife spoke to the thousands present, while outside the police endeavored to control the even larger numbers surrounding the buildings, yelling for Booth's blood. John Lawley sang a song that he had written himself, "My sins rose as high as a mountain." His fine tenor voice thrilled his hearers, and made Booth reflect that songs of a very different nature had been sung from that same stage just a few months before.

The significance of the day had not escaped the General. Capturing the devil's stronghold was a major triumph over Satan. Victory tasted sweet. But the devil is not one to lie down when someone makes attacks on his principality. He fought back. Thus far his strategy had been the use of the mob. That having failed, he now decided to use the law.

Booth had attacked the liquor trade once too often. Now that powerful interest attacked him.

The lease of The Eagle Tavern had a mandatory clause that the leaseholder of that building should keep "an inn, tavern or public house." When first challenged on this Booth showed little concern, even though the Army's use of the property fitted none of the alternatives.

Legal action was taken against them, but the Court of Chancery ruled in the Army's favor, that the then present use of The Eagle was not a breach of the covenant, as there was nothing to stop the premises being used for the sale of alcoholic beverages again, when their lease expired.

However, the landlords, with the support of the breweries, decided to take the matter further to the Court of Queen's Bench. That court ruled against the Army.

So Booth, to counter this, decided to keep an "inn," and opened The Eagle as a temperance hotel with accommodation for seventy.

The executors then took action to recover both The Eagle and The Grecian on the grounds that that specific clause in the lease had been contravened. Indeed, in spite of Booth's attempts to run an "inn," it was still being broken, because no alcoholic drinks were available there.

Eventually, after a further court summons and appeal, the Army was unable to continue to use The Eagle, though The Grecian continued as a major center of Salvation Army activities until the lease expired in 1898.

24

The Army in India

*T*he Salvation Army's ranks were filling rapidly with an astonishing array of ex-drunks, converted convicts, saved prostitutes, and an assortment of soldiers from the poorest segments of society. The organization had attracted a few women of the "better classes," but not men. The first "gentleman" to join the ranks of the Army was Frederick St. George de Lautour Tucker. Tucker had been born in India in 1853, the son of a civil servant in the Raj.

The younger Tucker also joined the Indian civil service, but not before he had been converted at a crusade conducted by American evangelists Moody and Sankey in England. He was in Britain at that time, taking his civil service examinations.

While serving in India and evangelizing in his spare time, he came across a copy of the *War Cry*. He was so intrigued by it that he applied for leave, primarily to visit William Booth. He was impressed by his meeting with the General, and all he saw of this strange church made a great impact upon him. But he was not one to make hasty decisions. He investigated the organization for several months before resigning his position as Assistant-Commissioner at Amritsar and joining the Salvation Army. His civil service income had been nearly £500 per year. The Salvation Army guaranteed no income.

Booth, recognizing his ability, gave him the rank of Major and set him to work in the Legal Department at International Headquarters.

Tucker was delighted to have joined the ranks, but he had not joined to work in an office. He wanted a frontline posting. He was fluent in Hindustani and Urdu and was familiar with Sanskrit, and so his posting should obviously be to India. Obvious, that is, to Tucker. The General, overwrought by worries from three continents, was reluctant to add a fourth.

But Tucker put forth his case for an attack upon India convincingly, and Booth was never one to doubt for long when the salvation of souls was at stake.

Tucker arrived in Bombay in September 1882 with Captain Henry Bullard and Lieutenants Arthur Norman and Mary Thompson. They had let it be known that they would live in India like native Indians, even adopting native dress. When the news filtered through to their destination before their arrival, it was greeted with considerable disquiet among the English population.

They disembarked, the men wearing yellow lightweight coats stretching down to their knees, pantaloons, turbans, and boots. Lieutenant Thompson wore a yellow shawl covering most of her fair hair and shoulders, and an ankle-length yellow dress. They were greeted by a small group of missionaries of various denominations, and a considerably larger contingent of police.

The Superintendent of Police approached Tucker as he stepped on the quay. "Are you in charge of this 'army'?" he asked. He uttered the final word with contempt.

"Yes," said Frederick, "I'm Major Tucker."

"Where are the rest of your 'troops'?" demanded the Superintendent with the same contempt.

The Major hesitated. "They are all here," he said, indicating his three companions.

The policeman's mouth fell open at this revelation. He looked at his assembled constables and back to the heavily outnumbered Salvationists. "But we heard you were going to take India by storm. There must be more of you," he insisted.

"No, just us," confirmed Tucker.

The Superintendent was stunned. "We were expecting a thousand . . ." His voice trailed away. Recovering himself, he quickly rejoined his constables and smartly led them away from the dock.

The next day the Major was summoned before the Commissioner of Police. He stood before a large desk, behind which sat the Commissioner, Sir Frank Soutar.

"I want to make it clear that we will not tolerate any trouble from your organization, Mr. Tucker," he warned. "You are forbidden to hold any outdoor meetings or processions. Is that clear?"

Tucker's moustache bristled in anger, but he controlled himself. His legal knowledge was about to come in useful. "Commissioner, before joining the Salvation Army I was Assistant-Commissioner in Amritsar," he said calmly, "and I can assure you that there is nothing in the law to forbid us holding marches in Bombay's streets. Muslims and Hindus do, without let or hindrance, and we as Christians claim the same right."

It was now the Commissioner's turn to bristle. "Mr. Tucker," he said threateningly, "I do not like being defied. I forbid you to hold street marches, and if you try it we will make it hot for you."

Tucker left his antagonist's office and returned to his troops. He was reluctant to cause trouble and disobey the Commissioner's command, but felt he had a higher authority to obey. After a brief struggle of conscience, he led his three soldiers out on to the streets.

As the little parade of soldiers—with Bullard playing the cornet, Norman a drum, and Mary Thompson a tambourine—marched in one direction, another procession approached them. It was a long file of Hindus playing tom-toms, cymbals, and trumpets. The two columns passed each other with a discordant effect. As they moved away from the Indians, they became aware that a large force of police was blocking the way a few hundred yards ahead.

As they drew near to the policemen the Deputy Commissioner, John Smith, dismounted and called, "In the name of Her Majesty, Queen of England and Queen Empress of India, I order you to disperse!"

The Salvationists stopped. They could go no farther forward. Frederick Tucker raised his hand, and claimed his higher authority, "In the name of His Majesty, the King of kings and Lord of lords, I command you to stand aside!"

Smith was not impressed. He ordered his men to arrest the offenders and they were taken to the police station. The magistrate dismissed them with a caution, but when they appeared before him again the next day he fined Tucker £5 *or* two weeks' jail in default, and the others £2.10s or a week's incarceration. They all chose jail.

After their period in prison they started publishing two editions of the *War Cry*, one in English and the other in Gujarati, the local dialect.

The middle of October saw reinforcements arrive, including Mrs. Tucker. They worked hard to establish the Army in Bombay in spite of the continued official opposition, and with the extra personnel available were able to spread their activities to Calcutta and Lucknow. Most of their success was with the Indians. Their fellow Englishmen would have little to do with them, except to try to thwart their evangelistic efforts.

The Salvationists identified with the Indians thoroughly. Tucker insisted that they dress like them, live in similar conditions in the Indian parts of towns and not with their fellow Englishmen, cook and eat the same food, and wash their clothes side by side with the Indians in the rivers and streams.

With such dedication it seemed inevitable that the Army would grow, and grow it did. Tucker boldly appointed Indians and other Asians of ability to positions of rank in the Army. He was not afraid to place them over Europeans. He appointed Arnolis Weerasooriya, a young, balding Singhalese, as his second-in-command. The only complaints he received came from outside the organization. The Raj would never understand or sympathize with the Salvation Army.

Back in England the General received reports of the successes and sufferings in India with praise and thanksgiving, but with little sympathy. He had endured persecution himself, and believed that no Salvationist should expect otherwise.

25

A Salvationist Wedding

When Florence Soper returned from France early in 1882 she was stationed briefly at the new headquarters. Her intelligence and ability did not go unnoticed by the General. Her good looks and sweet nature did not go unnoticed by his son.

Bramwell by this time was a tall, good-looking twenty-six-year-old, with a jet-black beard, and no romantic entanglements. His position in the Army as second-in-command to his father made him very visible to the rank and file. Everybody noticed Bramwell, not least Florence Soper.

With both of them working at headquarters for a time, they began to get to know each other well. Knowledge grew to liking, liking to fondness, and fondness to love. The romance blossomed and, with the General's approval, the date was set for the wedding—Thursday, October 12, 1882.

Meantime, the General, with a mixture of delight and concern, had observed the marriage of numerous officers, and decided that a code of conduct was needed for those entering matrimony. He drew up seven articles to which both parties had to agree before he would consent to marry them. The directives included: "We promise never to allow our marriage to lessen in any way our devotion to God or to the Army," and "We promise always to regard and arrange our home in every way as Salvation Army Soldiers' (or Officers') quarters, and to train everyone in it to faithful service in the Salvation Army." Booth knew too well that marriage could come between a Christian and God.

Bramwell had no problems with such conditions, as he had

never known any other life. His attractive fiancee, likewise, saw no difficulty in concurring with her General's instructions. Though some officers may have questioned Booth's involvement in this area of their lives, the future Mr. and Mrs. Bramwell Booth did not.

The day of the wedding was set, but this did not deter thousands of well-wishers packing and surrounding the Congress Hall at Clapton. Neither were they discouraged by Booth's charging a shilling a head to attend the great occasion. He saw it as an excellent opportunity to reduce the debt on The Grecian and The Eagle Tavern.

The wedding was set for 11 A.M., but long before that the assembled throng was singing songs of praise and thanksgiving. At the appointed hour the brass band marched from the platform to the entrance of the hall, met the happy couple at the door and escorted them to the platform together. The bride's father was not present to give her away, as he still stubbornly opposed his daughter's involvement in the Army. The men and women in the crowded hall cheered and waved handkerchiefs as the uniformed couple walked toward the front of the hall.

Bramwell and Florence ascended the platform steps and came to a halt in front of the General. The cheers and shouts of "Praise the Lord!" and "Hallelujah!" rang out. The people seemed reluctant to cease. Finally the bandmaster put a whistle to his lips and blew on it three times. Silence gradually settled over the hall.

Booth had enjoyed the delay. But now silence reigned and he began the service. "Let us sing," he called out, "the second hymn on the song sheet: *Come, Savior Jesus, from above; Assist me with Thy heavenly grace.*" The band played the introduction and the congregation exploded into song.

When the hymn had finished, Booth addressed the crowd. "This is a great day," he began, "a happy occasion. Yet there is something in life that is a greater guarantee of happiness than marriage. It is salvation from sin in and through the Lord Jesus Christ. If any in this hall today do not know the Lord Jesus, I urge you to come and get married to Him, and then you'll have a honeymoon that will last for life, and will never get sour." Cries of "Amen" greeted the General's assertion.

"Amen!" echoed Booth. "What a great sound! But you can do better than that. All those who enjoy their religion shout,

'Amen!' " commanded the showman-General.

The crowd erupted into deafening obedience, as shouts of "Amen!" came from all parts of the hall. Then gradually the hub-bub declined into silence.

The General turned to his son and the bride. Of his son he enquired, "You've not been married before, I suppose?" Booth did not joke often, but the crowd enjoyed that one. Bramwell smiled nervously, and licked his dry lips.

Booth addressed the congregation again, "Dearly beloved, we are gathered here in the sight of Almighty God, to join together this man and this woman in holy matrimony."

The service continued. The bride and groom said their vows. A ring, a Salvationist's solitary concession to jewelry, was placed on Florence's third finger, and she became Mrs. Bramwell Booth.

At the end of the service William Booth spoke to the happy crowd again. "I am sometimes asked, 'General, what will happen when you die? Who will take your place?' Well, the generalship of the Salvation Army is not a hereditary position, but I believe it is not just possible, but probable that my son Bramwell would take my place." Cheers went up from the faithful. The General smiled.

"Should he do so," continued Booth, "I believe that there would rally round him the hearts of the tens of thousands in this organization that have rallied round me." Cheers and applause rose from the gathering. Bramwell was popular and respected.

Catherine, the Army "Mother," followed by Bramwell's great friend George Railton, then addressed the happy congregation, and as the celebrations slowly died down, the newly married couple slipped away for a brief honeymoon.

26

Ministry to Prostitutes

*B*ecause of the nature of their work it had been part of the Salvation Army's lot to have contact with prostitutes from the early days. Indeed Catherine Booth's first encounter with them was in 1865, when she addressed a meeting organized by the Midnight Movement, a group founded to reclaim and rehabilitate prostitutes.

Over the years many of their stations had had street girls kneel at their penitent benches. In some cases they did not return to their trade and joined the Army, but in others they did fall back, some out of economic hardship. There was no formal way of helping them after conversion, other than the general Army method of putting them to work in the Army's service in whatever job was available.

In 1881 a Salvationist named Elizabeth Cottrill was the first to make a consistent attempt to tackle the problem. At the end of one of the Sunday services she was counseling a prostitute. She became a Christian that night, but a whole new problem arose. She could not go back to the brothel which had been her home for some time, but she had nowhere else to go. Mrs. Cottrill discussed the problem with one of the officers, as the girl sat on the penitent bench crying. They talked about the difficulty, and it was not finally resolved until the motherly Mrs. Cottrill decided that the young woman would have to go home with her.

She took her charge home, put her in her own bed, and slept on the couch herself. When her husband, a night-worker on the newspapers and not a Salvationist, came home he was informed of the situation and, with remarkable tolerance, took his wife's place on the couch, while the visitor still slept in the upstairs room.

The reclaimed prostitute was soon reunited with her family in another town. But now Mrs. Cottrill had the bit firmly between her teeth, and let it be known that any harlot wishing to change her ways could live in one of her two basements until they were able to find other accommodation. The patient Mr. Cottrill—and their five children—supported his wife in her crusade, but not always with enthusiasm.

On one occasion Elizabeth Cottrill hurried to the door when she heard loud cries out in the street. As she opened her door she was confronted by a man and a woman struggling, the woman screaming and the man threatening her with a knife. The bold Elizabeth lunged forward and pushed the man aside, grabbed hold of the woman, pulled her inside the house, then shut and locked the door. The man banged on the door for an hour before he gave up and left. The Salvationist gave her newfound lodger, who was shaking violently, the usual Cottrill treatment—bath, food, and bed.

The woman's antagonist returned frequently while his "woman" stayed with the Cottrills, and he made all kinds of threats. She was eventually placed as a maid in northern England and escaped her persecutor.

Finally Mr. Cottrill's patience ran out. "My dear Elizabeth," he said stoutly one day, "for three years I and the children have tolerated the invasion of our home by a string of young women of doubtful morals, but now it must end. For the children's sake we cannot ignore the danger they represent. You have brought home your last fallen woman."

The next day Elizabeth Cottrill went to see Bramwell Booth at headquarters in Queen Victoria Street. She was ushered into his modest office, and with tears in her eyes told her story.

Bramwell sat listening intently, his eyes fixed on hers. Every now and then he would move slightly in his chair, or nervously stroke his beard. He was greatly impressed by her sincerity, and deeply moved by her story. Word of the project had reached his ears before, but not in such detail. He was previously unaware of the extent of the commitment of this remarkable woman and the scope of her work.

She finished her tale in desperation. "What can I do, Mr.

Booth? Where can these poor women go now? There's nowhere for them."

Bramwell rose from his chair, walked over to the window and looked out at the busy street. He thought for a while. Mrs. Cottrill sat, endlessly wiping her eyes with an already damp handkerchief.

"Mrs. Cottrill," said the Chief-of-Staff, turning to the distraught woman, "tell your husband not to worry. We do understand his predicament and we don't blame him in any way." He paused for a moment. "I think I might also have the solution to our problem. Would you be agreeable to finding a suitable house for this work, and run it on the Army's behalf? We would, of course, pay all the expenses."

Mrs. Cottrill raised her head and looked at Bramwell as if to see if he really meant it, her eyes still wet with tears. "Oh! Mr. Booth," she said excitedly, realizing that he did, "I would. Yes, I would. Oh, Mr. Booth, that is truly an answer to prayer. I will start looking right away."

She rose from her seat and made to go toward the door, then turned back to Bramwell. "I'm sorry, Mr. Booth. I am forgetting my manners. Thank you. Thank you very much. I will let you know when I have a suitable place." She turned again and walked toward the door.

Two days later she had rented a three-story house in nearby Hanbury Street and started her work.

27

Fighting Child Abuse

*E*arly in 1885 the caretaker of the International Headquarters, Major William Fenny, opened the front doors one morning and discovered a teenage girl sitting on the doorstep. The girl, clad in a scarlet silk dress, sprang to her feet at Fenny's appearance and told the surprised man, "I want to see General Booth."

"Can I help you, my deary?" said the Major kindly. "The General isn't here yet."

"No!" said the girl. "I must see General Booth."

"Well, you had better wait inside," he said, ushering her into the entrance hall and directing her to a seat. "Just sit there, miss, and I'll get you a cup of tea."

Later the girl agreed to see Bramwell Booth, as the General had unexpectedly gone to one of the Army Halls and would not be available till much later. She told Bramwell a horrifying story.

"My name's Annie Swan, Mr. Booth," she said. "I'm a good girl."

Bramwell did not argue.

"I come from Sussex, Mr. Booth," she began her story. "I used to go to Salvation Army meetings there. I answered an advertisement for a maid position in Pimlico, and arrived in London last week. When I reached the address I met the lady who had replied to my application, but, Mr. Booth"—her speech became more agitated—"they didn't want me as a maid at all. They wanted me . . ." She hesitated, looked at Bramwell and away again. "They wanted me to . . . Oh! Mr. Booth!" she exclaimed, catching his eye and then looking away yet again.

Bramwell felt his stomach churn as her meaning dawned on him. "I think I understand, my dear," he interrupted. "Can you continue?"

She paused as she calmed herself, then she continued, "I was locked in a room, Mr. Booth, and was told that I had to be a 'lady' like the other girls in the house. But I'm a good girl, Mr. Booth.

"Last evening they took me downstairs to see this man." She paused again. "He wasn't nice, Mr. Booth. He said things, and tried to grab hold of me, so I pushed him away and ran. I hid in the kitchen and pushed the table and some cupboards up against the door so no one could get in. I heard the lady I had met say, 'Leave her there till morning. She'll come to her senses when she wants her breakfast.' During the night I crept back to my room, found my *Salvation Army Song Book*"—she raised the red covered book so that Bramwell could see it—"looked for General Booth's address and came here. I'm not going back there, Mr. Booth, and they've got my things."

Bramwell had listened intently to the seventeen-year-old's story. Anger seethed within him. He remained outwardly calm. "Worry no further, my dear. You are safe with us. We will make sure no harm comes to you." He rose and paused reflectively. Then he said, "I will introduce you to one of our lady officers, who will look after you until you are able to go back home. I will then arrange for your luggage to be collected. Just wait a moment."

He left the room and in a few minutes returned with Florence Booth. "Miss Swan, this is my wife. She will look after you now. God bless you," he said.

Florence took the girl's hand and helped her from the chair. "Would you like some breakfast, Annie?" she asked, putting her arm around the girl.

"Oh yes, Mrs. Booth. I haven't eaten anything for ages," replied the girl, her spirits rising.

Florence led the girl from the office and Bramwell sat down heavily in his chair. He put his head in his hands as the tears of anger and frustration welled up and ran down his cheeks and into his beard. He stayed in that position for half an hour, reflecting and praying. Then he rose, left his office, sought out an officer and gave him the address with instructions to collect the young woman's luggage.

The officer went to the house in Pimlico, where a woman at first refused to let him have the trunk. The officer made it quite clear that if she did not part with it, the next officer on her doorstep would be a police constable. The brothel keeper relented after that threat, and Annie Swan's luggage was retrieved.

Florence Booth, at the suggestion of the General, had been working at the hostel for reclaimed prostitutes for a few months when the Annie Swan incident occurred. Three months later she was the catalyst in a matter which hit the headlines and took the country by storm.

The Chief-of-Staff's wife was in charge of the home in Hanbury Street begun by Mrs. Cottrill, who still worked there. One night Florence Booth returned to her home in Castlewood Road, Clapton (a borough just north of the main sphere of Army activities), greatly distressed. When Bramwell arrived home his wife was sobbing convulsively on their bed, with their toddler Catherine in her cot screaming for attention, unheeded.

Bramwell rushed to his wife, comforted her, and tried to discover the reason for her anguish. Her crying continued, but on two occasions when she managed to catch her breath sufficiently to speak she just said, "I can't tell you."

Little Catherine persisted in trying to get her share of the attention, and eventually gained a little from her normally doting father.

Florence would not be comforted. She also obstinately refused to tell the reason for her distress, and spent the night in a highly emotional state and slept little.

For the next two days she traveled with her infant daughter to Hanbury Street in a daze, helped look after the twelve charges there, and returned home in a state of misery. Both evenings Bramwell found her crying. Both nights she hardly slept. Her tears continued to soak the sheets.

Bramwell also slept little. The third morning he was lying on the couch in the parlor, trying to gain some undisturbed sleep, when his wife came down from the bedroom. As he saw her enter the room he sat up, looked at her but said nothing.

Florence was calm now, but her face showed the marks of her distress. Her normally serene features were marred. Her eyes were red and the areas below them swollen. Her cheeks were stained by her tears. She walked slowly to the couch as if in a trance, and sat down next to Bramwell.

For a while neither spoke. Then Florence whispered, "It's too horrible."

Her husband's hearing impediment prevented him catching the words, but he could read the feeling of distaste on her face. He did not speak.

She gazed into nothingness as, falteringly, she began to tell the reason for her emotional upheaval. "Children, Bramwell, children!" she said vaguely.

Bramwell heard this time but failed to understand. He remained silent. There was a pause that seemed like an age to him.

"Girls, thirteen and fourteen years of age," she said and stopped again. She continued, "Young girls, seduced and . . . and . . . imprisoned for the most awful reasons." Her sheltered upbringing had not prepared her for anything like that.

Bramwell heard and understood. He moved to put his arm around his wife, but she pushed it away, as if at this terrible time the whole male sex, even her husband, stood condemned in her eyes, because of the appalling deeds of the few.

"On the streets they are—girls of thirteen and fourteen. Watched over by their seducers so that they cannot escape," she said more strongly.

She paused again, then continued, "We have three of them at the refuge, Bramwell." She looked at him for the first time, but hurriedly averted her eyes. "Three of them, all under sixteen they are. It's horrible, Bramwell. Horrible!" she exclaimed, her voice rising in volume and pitch. "We must do something!"

Silence returned for a few moments, then Bramwell spoke. "Are you sure, Florrie? I mean, are they really that young?"

Florence Booth turned to her husband with that kind of look that even the most saintly of wives reserve for their husbands when their word is doubted. "Yes, Bramwell, they are children," she explained.

"Maybe they are exaggerating or even lying," offered her unbelieving spouse.

"No, Bramwell, they fell into the same trap as Annie Swan, and we know what nearly happened to her," responded the wife firmly.

The shades of doubt covering his mind's eye slowly vanished, and for the first time Bramwell understood his wife's distress. "Then, Florrie, we must indeed do something. Get Catherine and we will go to the refuge immediately. I want to speak to those poor girls," he said, snapping into action.

They arrived at Hanbury Street before most of the occupants were up. Bramwell duly interviewed the three children. They told their disturbing story in a manner that left him in no doubt as to its truth, and that they were not unique. As he listened he was already forming the skeleton of a plan to attack this detestable trade.

28

Gathering Evidence

*T*he Salvation Army was not the only organization that was working to save prostitutes. Nor were they the first to become aware of child prostitution. Josephine Butler, the wife of an eminent Anglican clergyman, had organized a petition in 1881 which urged that action be taken to ban such practices. The petition, signed by over 1,000 women in the upper echelons of society, was presented to the Prime Minister. It read:

> That such changes ought to be made in the English laws as shall make it impossible for any young girl or child in our country to be deprived of her liberty by fraud or force, and to be kept in a foreign city in bondage for the basest purposes.

As reported in the petition, there was definite evidence that some unfortunates were actually taken overseas to be exploited by their unscrupulous "owners." The petition achieved nothing concrete. What was needed was something more sensational than a piece of paper signed by 1,000 ladies, however eminent.

Cases of juvenile prostitution, including children even younger than the Booths had encountered, were common. People taken to court for forcing youngsters into such a terrible kind of life most often escaped punishment, because of the weakness of the law. The age of consent at this stage was thirteen, and the usual defence for anyone caught with a teenage prostitute was, "She consented."

A Royal Commission set up to investigate the matter in 1871 had reported that in a period of eight years in three London hospitals nearly 3,000 cases of venereal disease had been discovered among girls between the ages of eleven and sixteen. Most of them were prostitutes.

Ten years later a Select Committee had been established by the House of Lords to look into the scandal, and it included such notables as the Prime Minister (W. E. Gladstone), the Archbishop of Canterbury, and Lord Shaftesbury. The committee confirmed the worst and a bill, based on their recommendations, was passed by the House of Lords in 1883. Astonishingly, it was rejected by the House of Commons. This was repeated in 1884, and a year later, when the bill was debated for a third time, it was again rejected.

It is a sad fact that many politicians, of yesterday and today, are more readily moved by public opinion than by conscience. Public opinion had to be stirred.

Bramwell Booth set out to discover as much as he could about this infamous trade, and met with Mrs. Butler and others who had actively campaigned against it. He knew the answer lay in publicity. The public must be made aware of the iniquitous situation. The hands of the politicians must be forced to make that bill law. But how could he and the Army make enough noise to achieve that? Certainly, the movement was still growing rapidly, but they only represented a small percentage of the population and they were still frowned on by most sections of the community. What was needed was the support of a prominent journalist.

W. T. Stead, the editor of *The Pall Mall Gazette*, had been increasingly sympathetic to the Army and was becoming one of the most influential journalists of the period. Lord Fisher described him as "the greatest journalist of his day." Bramwell decided that Stead was his man.

He gained an interview with the editor, went to his office in Northumberland Avenue, and put forth his case. Stead sat in his chair. His eyes searched Bramwell's intently. His graying beard covered his chest, and his fingers drummed incessantly on his desk. Bramwell concluded, and Stead, disappointingly, was unimpressed. But Bramwell had a trump card to play. Outside the editor's office, waiting for the Salvationist's summons, were the three young girls he had met at Hanbury Street and a converted brothel keeper named Rebecca Jarrett.

Bramwell suggested that Stead might like to interview the

girls in question. He reluctantly agreed. The four nervous females were ushered into the book-lined office, and were offered chairs. Stead, halfheartedly at first, began to ask questions. As the answers came his interest picked up, and he began to scribble quickly upon a pad on his desk.

After the interview the women left the room, and the two men sat, silently facing each other across the desk. Stead's brow was creased in a worried frown. His fingers still drummed noisily on the tabletop. Suddenly, he raised his right hand, and brought his fist down hard on the desk with a bang and cursed.

Bramwell, shaken by the explosiveness of the outburst, was momentarily stunned. He recovered and countered, "Yes, that's all very well, but it will not help us. The first thing to do is to get the facts in such a form that we can publish them."

Stead had been won over. "Yes," he agreed, "give me all the information you have, and I will arrange meetings with some influential people likely to be sympathetic—Josephine Butler for one. Now there's a woman who it's hard to say no to! Ben Scott is another. He's bound to be with us on this. Yes, Bramwell Booth, we are going to make a noise—a noise that will rock the Empire!"

At Bramwell's suggestion they closed the discussion with a time of prayer.

Stead, true to his word, met with key people in various walks of life to gain information and support. Josephine Butler, by her own confession an "old political agitator," warned that to force Parliament's hand it was not enough to win support in London. The whole country had to be moved. What was needed was something most dramatic.

They thought and prayed and formed a plan. The idea was to procure a child themselves and send her to Salvationists in France to prove how easy it was, and then publish their findings.

Here they needed the expertise of Rebecca Jarrett. She was the thirteenth and final child in her family. Her father deserted them while she was still young, and her mother then turned to alcohol for solace. When Rebecca was only twelve her mother took her to the Cremorne Gardens in London's Chelsea, where a brothel operated. Rebecca went off with whatever man wanted her, while her mother counted the money. This went on for three years, until Rebecca decided that if she had to live that kind of

life then it was better that she make the money and not her
mother. So she left home and lived as a prostitute and then a
brothel-keeper until her mid-thirties.

She became sick, mainly through excessive alcohol, and
moved to Northampton. While there she saw a sign that read:

SALVATION ARMY
GREAT DOINGS LED BY THE
HALLELUJAH CLERGYMAN
& THE HALLELUJAH SWEEP.
GREAT FIRING BY GREAT GUNS!

Secretly she went to one of the meetings that was held in an
abandoned prison. The "Hallelujah Sweep," Elijah Cadman, was
his usual uninhibited self. He was prancing around the platform
preaching earnestly to the lost, the sweat pouring from his brow.
It was a hot evening and Rebecca, already feeling sick, was overcome by the oppressive conditions and fainted while Cadman
preached. The Salvationists, thinking they had another convert,
surrounded her. She slowly came to. Captain Susan "Hawker"
Jones (she acquired that nickname because she used to help her
father in his rat-catching business) spoke with her and discovered
that her "convert" was only interested in getting home.

Rebecca refused to allow herself to be taken home by two of
the "Hallelujah Lasses," not because she was ashamed of living
in a brothel, but rather that she was ashamed to be seen in the
company of these odd religious folk.

Next day Captain Jones, who had suspicions about the kind
of work Jarrett was engaged in, went looking for her. It was
obvious that the brothel-keeper was very sick, and the Captain
offered to take her to a doctor. Rebecca, having now overcome
her fears of being seen with a Salvationist, assented. The doctor
examined her, instructed that she should be confined to bed, and
said she required constant nursing. The bed was "Hawker" Jones'
and the nursing was done by Salvationists.

The patient was amazed at the kindness she received, and
continually reflected that "they are doing it for nothing."

When she had sufficiently recovered they moved her to London, to the Hanbury Street home, where she was greeted by
Mrs. Cottrill with a kiss.

She received visits from Catherine Booth, and Florence spent a great deal of time with her, counseling her on her drink problem and praying with her. It was in the General's own home that Rebecca Jarrett eventually came to the Lord.

Her early Christian experience was a struggle, and she went to live with Canon and Josephine Butler for a time. They proved to be an enormous strength and encouragement to her. She later opened up her own refuge for young girls, which was a remarkably successful project.

Rebecca Jarrett was the obvious choice as Bramwell's "procuress," and she was invited to meet with the Chief-of-Staff at International Headquarters. Bramwell's plan was explained to her. She was shocked.

"But I don't want to do it," she asserted. "I'm done wiv all that, Mr. Booth."

"But no harm will come to the girl. We will see to that," assured Bramwell.

"It will bring back too many memories, Mr. Booth. Please don't ask me to do that," she pleaded.

"I'm sorry, Rebecca, but I must. We believe that the law can be changed and children saved from this dreadful business, but we need your help," he insisted.

The woman bit her bottom lip as she considered the problem. Her face was etched with strain as she agonized over the decision. Reluctantly she conceded. "All right, Mr. Booth. I'll buy a child for you."

"Thank you, Rebecca," said the relieved Salvationist. "We will do our best to see that it causes you as little pain as possible."

Bramwell then went to visit Stead, and they wrote a carefully worded letter outlining the plan which was to be sent to the Archbishops of Canterbury and London, Cardinal Manning, and several members of Parliament. The letters were to be posted before the act took place, but timed so that they would arrive immediately after it. This way, it was hoped, they would be safeguarded against charges of improper conduct.

Then Rebecca Jarrett was instructed to find a suitable child. She, true to her word, bought Eliza Armstrong for £2. Her mother parted with her with no questions asked and spent her ill-gotten gains in the nearest pub.

The girl was then taken to another procuress named Madame Mourez, who certified that Eliza was a virgin. She was then taken to a brothel where W. T. Stead had acquired a room. Eliza entered Stead's room in a state of nervous bewilderment. The newspaper editor did his best to put her at ease during the hour and a quarter she spent with him.

Eliza was then "rescued" by Captain Caroline Reynolds who took her to a doctor to confirm that she had not been violated. The next day she was whisked away to Paris with Lieutenant Elizabeth Combe, who had been serving with the Army in Europe.

They now had all the evidence they needed. They had shown that a girl could be bought from her parents, taken to a brothel, left with a prospective customer, and then taken away to another land.

29

The Storm Breaks

On Monday, July 6, 1885, the storm broke. The first of four articles appeared on the front page of *The Pall Mall Gazette*.

"Maiden Tribute to Modern Babylon!" shouted the newsboys, echoing the paper's headlines. "Sensational revelations!"

The first article told the story of Lily (Eliza Armstrong) and her abduction. Then the paper exposed the trade in children for prostitution.

The reception the paper received was even more sensational than the report. News got around quickly about the nature of the news, and crowds gathered around the hassled newsboys to pay a penny for a copy. By the afternoon the papersellers, realizing the potential gold mine in their hands, put the price up and up and up. The final copies sold for half-a-crown, thirty times their original value.

The subject became (discreetly, of course) the nation's main talking point, but opinion was divided. Some were greatly angered by what they saw as little more than sensationalism, and by the method used to acquire the information. During the afternoon a crowd began to collect outside the offices of *The Pall Mall Gazette*. They were wanting blood—Stead's blood. That night Stead required police protection to get home.

The next day a larger printing of the second issue was published. It had the same effect as its predecessor. It sold out entirely.

That afternoon a tall young man broke through the crowd that had gathered again in Northumberland Avenue, and after scrutiny by the police constables guarding the *Gazette's* offices, went up the stairs to see Stead's secretary. The secretary entered Stead's office. "Excuse me, Mr. Stead. There is a gentleman to see you."

"I've told you I can't see anyone at the moment. I'm too busy," said the editor, who was anxiously pacing up and down.

"He's very persistent, sir. He won't go away. He says he must see you," informed the woman.

"Who is he?" Stead asked impatiently.

"Shaw is his name, sir—George Bernard Shaw. He says he's a writer. He's Irish," she added with obvious distaste. "He won't go away until he's seen you, Mr. Stead."

"Very well, then," consented the longsuffering editor, "let him come in."

The secretary left the room and returned with the visitor. Stead noticed the twinkle in his eye as the two shook hands. "Mr. Stead," said Shaw, "I want to congratulate you on a courageous piece of journalism."

Stead directed him to a chair. "Thank you, Mr. Shaw. I wish everyone felt the way you do." He walked to the window and peered out. "There are many out there who seem prepared to put my courage further to the test."

"There will always be those who oppose men and women who do right. Did they not crucify Christ?" encouraged the playwright.

"W. H. Smith and Sons have banned the *Gazette*. They refuse to sell it again," lamented Stead, turning to his visitor. "One of our main distributors gone. They call it obscene."

"Obscene is it? What it exposes is obscene, Mr. Stead." Shaw paused for a moment, then continued. "Mr. Stead, you have two more issues to run on this scandal; is that correct?"

Stead nodded.

"Then tomorrow and Thursday I will collect as many quire of the paper as I can carry, and I will sell them for you," offered the writer. "I believe I can rally some friends who will help, too," he added.

Stead smiled for the first time that day. "Thank you, Mr. Shaw. Your offer is gladly accepted. We will win this battle. We will change that law!"

"I will delay you no longer," said Shaw, rising. "Good day to you, Mr. Stead."

They shook hands again, and the Irishman turned and left the office.

The third and fourth issues were duly published, and George Bernard Shaw was true to his word.

The other newspapers were highly critical of the campaign, as were many people of note, but as the week progressed public opinion swung very strongly in favor of Stead and his conspirators. As the tide of supportive public opinion swelled, the newspapers changed their tune, becoming less critical and then mildly sympathetic.

The members of Parliament at first took scant notice of what they considered little more than a stunt, but as the public began to demand action it was decided to resurrect the previously defeated Criminal Law Amendment Bill.

While the leaders of the nation prepared to debate the matter, the Salvation Army mobilized and began holding meetings up and down the country to continue to draw attention to it. Catherine Booth addressed a rally for ladies only at a hall in Piccadilly on July 13. The next day she joined with Josephine Butler and other public figures to present their case to a mixed audience. The General, who had had considerable doubts about the wisdom of the campaign, threw his weight behind it. He traveled rapidly around northern England lecturing in support of the cause.

Catherine also wrote to Queen Victoria to enlist her aid. She received a reply from the Dowager Marchioness of Ely. It read in part: "Her Majesty has been advised that it would not be desirable for the Queen to express any opinion upon a matter which forms at present the object of a measure before Parliament."

A petition was organized by the Army and gained nearly 400,000 signatures. It took eight Salvationists to carry it to the House of Commons. It was escorted, with typical Salvation Army flair, by a long parade of soldiers including a band of fifty from the Congress Hall in Clapton.

The government had only been in office a month and was acutely embarrassed by an issue its members wished would just go away. The Home Secretary decided to swim with the tide, and he invited Stead and Bramwell to make proposals to

121

strengthen the bill before it was put before Parliament.

In August the bill was debated. It was approved and, among other matters, the age of consent was raised to sixteen.

Victory had been achieved.

30

Opposition Mounts

To win a battle is not necessarily to win the war, and the enemy now fought back. On August 31 charges were laid against W. T. Stead, Bramwell Booth, Rebecca Jarrett, Louise Mourez, and Elizabeth Combe for "procuring a girl for immoral purposes."

The General was distraught. This could destroy the Army. The fears that he had had at the outset of this crusade were seemingly justified.

In the conduct of any campaign, of whatever nature, mistakes are made. The mistake that triggered off the decision to prosecute was Stead's publication of a letter from Lily to her mother, which had gone undelivered. The letter quoted an unusual rhyme, which Eliza's mother, upon reading the *Gazette,* recognized and so realized that Lily was in fact her Eliza.

Mrs. Armstrong took the matter to the press, complaining that Bramwell and Stead had abducted her child. The *Pall Mall Gazette's* rivals had a field day. Here was their chance to get even. Accusations of abduction against the two appeared in several headlines.

The matter was taken up by Cavendish Bentinck, a member of Parliament, who had strongly opposed the passing of the bill, and he pressed for legal action.

The Salvationist and the editor were finally summoned to Bow Street Court to the preliminary hearing. Upon leaving the court Bramwell was attacked by a mob and had to be rescued by the police.

At the end of October their trial began at the Old Bailey. They were tried under a law that had been enacted twenty-four years before, which did make it possible, in certain circumstances, for a procurer to be brought before the courts. Ironically, they were the first to be so summoned. The presiding judge was Mr. Justice Lopes, who seemed hostile to the defendants from the beginning.

It was agreed quite early in the trial that Elizabeth Combe had no case to answer, and she was acquitted. The case against Bramwell was also dismissed, to the General's heartfelt relief. The others were not so fortunate.

The Archbishop of Canterbury was present, on behalf of the defense, to testify that he had received a letter from Stead advising of the intended "crime," posted before it took place. The judge, however, did not allow him to be called, as he did not consider the motive relevant.

Rebecca Jarrett, who lied in court to cover up her murky past, underwent a vigorous cross-examination by the Attorney General. She eventually broke down and admitted her deceit in tears.

The trial concluded after thirteen days. Jarrett and Stead were found guilty of "feloniously abducting a child, one Eliza Armstrong." Jarrett and Stead were also found guilty of aiding and abetting an indecent assault committed on Armstrong by Madame Mourez (the examination to prove that she was a virgin). Jarrett and Mourez were given six months' imprisonment, Mourez with hard labor, and Stead became prisoner #245 for three months.

When Rebecca Jarrett had completed her sentence, she continued to work for the Salvation Army in the refuge homes. She remained a Salvationist and was "promoted to Glory" in 1928. W. T. Stead, it was said, was never quite the same man again.

General Booth was still concerned that the trial would have a detrimental effect on the Army, even though his son had been acquitted. If anything, the opposite proved to be the case. Though it may have been true that the perpetration of this "foul deed" may have technically broken the law, it was generally agreed that the motives of Stead, Bramwell, and their companions were admirable. The "Maiden Tribute to Modern Babylon" venture proved to be the first step in the Salvation Army becoming recognized as a worthy organization. The publicity had benefitted the Army greatly.

No wonder the relieved General wrote in the *War Cry*, "Now

then for a private thanksgiving for deliverance. Let us fill the land with Hallelujahs! Now for personal reconsecration and increased devotion to the work, not only for saving girls, but the boys and the fathers and the mothers from sin and perdition."

William Booth was on the attack again. He was always ready to press home the Gospel message when opportunity presented itself.

31

The General in North America

*T*he second wedding in the Booth household was that of
Ballington, by then a Colonel, to Maud Charlesworth.
They were married on Thursday, September 16, 1886.
The General increased the charge of the wedding breakfast to
2s. 6d!

The next day William Booth departed on his first trip overseas. He embarked on the *Auranic,* bound for New York, to
inspect his American and Canadian forces.

For years his critics had said he would one day flee the country
with the fortune they assumed he had been making from "fleecing
the poor." With the timing of his departure coming so soon after
the well-attended, high-priced wedding feast, the rumors increased. *That is the last we will see of William Booth,* thought
many.

But though Booth was not adverse to making money for his
Army, he had no desires for personal wealth. His trip to America
was for the Army's good, and he was to return three months
later.

Major Thomas E. Moore, Railton's successor as commander
of the American contingent, proved to be an unwise choice. At
first he did a splendid job and the work expanded rapidly. But on
being challenged by the General about his poor administration and
questionable handling of finances, he decided to conduct a war of
independence. He founded his own army, taking many of Booth's
corps and soldiers with him.

Other officers were sent from England under the leadership of Major Frank Smith at the end of 1884 to try to retrieve the situation. Smith threw himself into the task and achieved much, but to many of the American troops Booth was a distant figure. Why should American Salvationists take orders from him? What made him so special?

Gradually it dawned upon Smith that it was necessary for the General to visit America, and he suggested this to International Headquarters. It was some time before Bramwell recognized the wisdom of the request, but it was not long after that he was able to convince his father that a trip to America was essential for the success of the work there.

So Booth chose James Dowdle to accompany him, and set off across the Atlantic. The scene that greeted Booth and Dowdle when docking in New York was quite different from that which met Railton and his helpers over six years before. The newly erected Statue of Liberty boldly welcomed visitors, temporary and permanent alike, to the United States of America. The festivities organized to celebrate its dedication later in October had already begun. The whole area was festooned with decorations. And when they disembarked, instead of being stared at by a handful of onlookers and curiosity-seekers, they were greeted by hundreds of cheering Salvationists.

If the welcome from his soldiers was warm, that from the press was hot. The next day the newspapers made accusations that the recent marriage of Ballington and Maud Charlesworth was purely to obtain Miss Charlesworth's inheritance, she being the daughter of a well-to-do clergyman. Booth was used to being libelled, and he elected not to defend himself, reasoning that those who trusted him would continue to do so, those who did not never would.

From New York they went to Boston, where he addressed a gathering of free churchmen. In England, many Protestant parsons were indifferent to Booth and others downright antagonistic. Here he was received with great warmth by nearly all, and they enthused over his powerful preaching. Hundreds had to be turned away from crowded meetings in Chicago.

He was impressed everywhere by the enthusiasm of his troops, but also grew more and more concerned about the lack of adequate leadership. Though recognizing the ideal of leading the American Army with American officers, he knew that some would have to come from England if only in the short term. He wrote to Bramwell, "Oh, for some officers for this country. Staff. Staff. Staff! is wanted!"

After preaching to enthusiastic audiences in other American cities the two crossed the border into Canada. Booth was greatly impressed by the wide open spaces of Canada but concerned about what he considered its inadequate population. He filed the information in his mind for future reference.

Booth's three-month trip had been highly successful. He had healed much of the damage caused by the rift two years before and had gained the respect of his American and Canadian troops. He had also seen hundreds of souls saved and his own vision of where God was leading the Army had been enlarged. He arrived back in England on Christmas Day.

In April the following year Ballington and Maud Booth were appointed as leaders of the North American command.

32

Sleeping Under Bridges

General Booth was returning home late at night in December 1887. His cab had just crossed London Bridge, and as he looked through the window he saw a sight that shocked him. Beneath the approaches of the bridge about twenty figures sat huddled together for warmth. Booth looked back and noticed that they all appeared to be men.

"Why are they spending the night there?" he asked himself. "Nowhere else to go, I suppose, except the workhouses, and no one in their right mind would go to one of those places."

The notorious workhouses had been the official answer to poverty for the whole of Victoria's reign. The Poor Law of 1834, which had introduced them, was based on the principle, "If the poor are made miserable, then the poor will decrease in number." To that end conditions in the workhouses were terrible. Families were broken up, food was poor and limited, work was hard and long, and the organization was regimented and oppressive. Stories of the ill-treatment of inmates were common. Henry Stanley, the explorer, had lived in a workhouse as a boy. While there another lad was beaten so severely by a teacher that he died. No action was taken. The red-brick buildings that sprang up throughout Britain housed an institution feared and detested by the working class.

It was no wonder that many of the homeless preferred to sleep under the bridges or in the parks. At least they had their freedom and a dim light of hope, which the workhouse would certainly extinguish.

Booth's emotions were stirred. He arrived home, now at Clapton near his son, but did not go to bed as he did not wish to disturb his sick wife. He lay down on the couch in the parlor, but the thought of what he had witnessed gave him no peace. He was unable to sleep.

Before breakfast next morning Bramwell called to see his father on Army business. He was taken aback by the General's condition. His white hair and beard were in wild disarray. He was pacing the room in agitation, his hands clasped behind his back.

He looked at Bramwell and barked, "Bramwell, do you know that fellows are sleeping out at night under the bridges? All night on the stone? And in this weather!"

"Yes, General," replied his son. "Didn't you know that? I thought everybody knew that." It was surprising that Booth had not previously been aware of it.

"You knew that," came back the General accusingly, "and you haven't done anything about it?"

"Well, General," replied the younger man defensively, "we can't do everything. We just don't have the manpower. What with the rapid spread of the Army internationally, the growth of the work among fallen women, and the demands made upon us from so many quarters, our staff is spread pretty thinly. Then there is no finance. We don't have the money."

The General listened to his son's explanations silently. Bramwell continued, "And there is much more being done for the poor now, General. There are many organizations and individuals doing this kind of work."

As Bramwell concluded, his father sighed deeply. A short silence followed. Then the General looked at his son and said, "But, Bramwell, there are still men sleeping out in winter under the bridges. Do something, Bramwell! Do something! Something must be done. Get a warehouse or the like to house them. Make sure they have a roof over their heads and walls to keep the wind off. Don't pamper them though, Bramwell. Pampering never did any good for anybody."

It all sounded so simple, yet Bramwell knew it would be difficult. But a command was a command, and act he must. "Yes, General, I will do my best." So saying he turned and left his parents' home, quite forgetting the original purpose of his visit.

Bramwell began the search for appropriate premises and found an old warehouse in the West India Dock Road, Limehouse. There was only space to accommodate about seventy men, but at least it was a start. Facilities were installed to prepare and distribute soup and bread to others—men, women and children— for whom no space was available. The beds for the fortunate seventy were made from two benches lying on their side on either side of wool-stuffed leather mattresses in sheep-skin covers. The appearance of the beds had a remarkable resemblance to coffins, but no one complained. They were certainly more comfortable than the stone beds under London's bridges.

The men's home had been started as an act of faith. The money to pay for it was still not available at its opening. But in the January 21 issue of the *War Cry* Bramwell advised his troops of the venture and the need for funds. He wrote about the home and its location and aims, then ended with an appeal for its financial support. "But we find the alterations, fitting of the building, supply of steam apparatus, and other appliances will cost about £600. This we ask our friends to supply," pleaded the Chief-of-Staff.

T. A. Denny, a wealthy businessman who had helped with funding both the American and French invasions, contributed £100. The remainder came in quite quickly in smaller amounts.

Encouraged by the response, Bramwell's vision extended. He soon opened up other hostels in Clerkenwell and Marylebone. Then later in the year the old People's Mission Hall, for so long the center of their activities, was converted into another home.

So Bramwell did something, and the General did not shirk his duty either. Buzzing around in his mind was a project that would change the face of the Army, and finally make it acceptable to the general public. But before that plan became concrete, William's heart was to be torn asunder by a different matter.

33

Tragedy Strikes

*I*n 1887 both Emma and Eva Booth were seriously ill, and Catherine found time to nurse them even though she still undertook a long list of public engagements. As the year progressed, it became apparent that Catherine herself was not well. No stranger to ill health, she now grew weary more quickly, became more prone to fainting spells, and looked quite drawn and pale.

Early in February the next year, Catherine preached at the Colston Hall in Bristol at the end of a series of meetings over two days. She chose her text from 2 Samuel 24:13: "Advise and see what answer I shall return to him that sent us."

"God wants the answer," asserted Catherine. "What is the response which you, individually, will make to the voice that has been sounding in your ears during the last two days? You know it is the voice of God. It matters not what human instrument it has come through. Refusal to return an answer is an answer of defiance. It is saying back to God, 'Mind your own business. I don't want your will.' The voice is saying, 'Come to me. Bring that poor, stained, unbelieving, doubting soul of yours to me. I will empower you to walk before me as my beloved child, in holiness and righteousness all your days.' "

Her closing words were to ring in her own mind for weeks and months after. "Will you rise up, and say in your heart, 'Yes Lord, I accept, I submit.' "

She had to be helped from the platform after the exhausting public ministry. Then she was taken to an office at the back of the hall and helped onto a couch.

131

Shortly after returning to London, she became aware of a painful lump on her breast. She went to see her doctor, who made an appointment for her to visit a specialist, Sir James Paget.

She decided not to tell William until she knew the gravity of the situation, but needing the support of one member of the family, she informed Bramwell. He was stunned. He knew this could be very serious, and the thought of losing his mother was a very painful one.

"Have you seen a doctor?" he anxiously enquired.

"Yes, and I go to see a specialist tomorrow—Sir James Paget. They say he is the best in his field," replied Catherine.

"But mother, what if. . . ?" his question trailed off. He could feel the tears running down his cheeks. His throat was choked.

"Such matters must be left in the hands of the Lord, Bramwell. We are all in His hands," she replied.

"Does the General know?" he asked, sitting beside her and clasping her hands.

"No, Bramwell, and you must not tell him until we know the seriousness of my condition. We must not worry him unnecessarily."

"Are you sure that's wise, Mother," he asked.

"Yes, Bramwell, I insist. I will tell him after I have seen Dr. Paget," promised his mother.

Bramwell put his arms around her and held her close to him. His tears dripped on to her shoulder. He feared the worst. His mother was his greatest confidante and he had always been closer to her than any other member of the family.

The next day Catherine traveled to see the specialist at Hanover Square. Her husband knew only that she was going to the doctor, but though such trips were not rare, this one gave him a strange feeling of unease. But he buried such thoughts in the preparations he had to make for a trip to Holland later that day.

After the examination, the doctor confirmed the worst. "Mrs. Booth," he said slowly, "this tumor is of a cancerous type. I am afraid I will have to operate."

Catherine had determined that she would not submit to an operation.

"I will not be operated on, Sir James," she said firmly. "I know others who have had such an operation, and all it has done has increased their suffering. I am not afraid to meet the Lord's will."

"But an operation is your only chance, Mrs. Booth," he insisted earnestly.

"But not much of a chance though, Sir James, I am sure," she said softly. The specialist turned his head away from her gaze. "I will not let you perform this operation." She paused. Silence reigned for a minute or two, as the doctor declined to pursue the matter further.

"May I ask, Sir James, how long I have left?" she asked.

Paget looked at her and away again. "Well, I'm not sure that I could give a satisfactory estimate, Mrs. Booth," he said evasively.

"But you must have some idea," she persisted.

"It varies so much, Mrs. Booth," said the doctor, still trying to avoid being pinned down.

"I am not afraid to meet my Maker, Sir James. You have experience of these matters. You must be able to give me some idea," she insisted.

The doctor hesitated, and again looked at her and averted his glance. "Two years. Not more than two years," he said. "Every case is different, of course, but not more than two years."

Catherine remained calm; her hands were held tightly and still in her lap. "Thank you, doctor. I appreciate your honesty."

"If you change your mind about that operation, you must let me know straightaway, Mrs. Booth. The sooner it is done the better," advised the doctor as Catherine rose to leave.

"Oh, Mrs. Booth," he added, "please feel free to get a second opinion." He wrote on a piece of paper, and handed it to her. "Here are the names of two other doctors who know this field well. You may wish to see them."

"Thank you, Sir James," she said as she left the office. "God bless you."

As the horse-drawn cab wended its way homeward, Catherine fell on her knees and prayed. The tears, which had previously been held back, welled forth. Her emotions, so well under control earlier, now erupted. She prayed earnestly and tearfully—not for herself, but for her husband, her family, her Army. They needed her, and in two years she would be gone.

The cab pulled up outside their home, and her fifty-eight-year-old husband rushed down the stairs with surprising speed. The tears had now vanished and her face was wiped clean of their stains. She smiled wanly at him as he helped her down, and took her into the house.

She sat down, and as he stood nervously facing her she told him the bad news. It came as a bombshell. He sat down hard into a chair. His eyes glazed. He felt as though he were in an unreal world. His wife dying? How could that be? His soul's companion through so much trouble and joy for well over thirty years to leave him? It all seemed so strange, so unnatural.

Catherine rose from her chair, walked over to him and knelt beside him, taking his long, slender hands in hers. There were tears in her eyes.

The reality of the situation had dawned upon her husband. The news she had just imparted to him was the cold, savage truth. In two years his wife would no longer be by his side. He would be alone. How could he carry on alone? He needed her. Running this mushrooming Army with her help was difficult, without her it would be impossible.

"Do you know what was my first thought?" she asked gently. "That I should not be there to nurse you at your last hour."

He looked at her through a haze of tears. Taking his hands from hers, he put them tenderly around her shoulders, and kissed her forehead. "Oh, Kate," he whispered, but no other words came. He began to sob, and the tears wet his beard as they flooded down his cheeks.

Catherine comforted her husband and spoke of her confidence in the future of their family and their Army—a future she could share for only a little longer, but one she knew would be great.

Suddenly William sprang from his seat. "I must cancel my trip!" he said.

"No!" said Catherine rising slowly. "No! Go! It is your duty to go. You must go."

"But you need me," he stressed.

"My sickness must not interfere with God's work, William. You must go to Holland."

"Are you sure?" he questioned sensitively.

Catherine knew that what her husband needed more than anything at this moment was to throw himself, with his full, unbounded energy, into a demanding task. "Yes, William, I am sure. I want you to go."

So Booth went to Holland. On his way he stopped at the

International Headquarters to tell his eldest son about his mother's condition. They shared each other's grief, and knelt to pray together before the General left to visit his Dutch soldiers.

The *War Cry* of March 3, 1888, told the Army's rank and file the sad news.

On April 10 Emma married Frederick de Lautour Tucker, whose first wife had died fourteen months earlier in India.

Catherine spoke briefly at the wedding, and, though very ill, surprised every listener with her powerful message. One phrase stuck in the minds of most of her hearers: "You know we all have a world to give up." Catherine had long since given it up in a metaphoric sense, but they knew unless a miracle happened, she was to give it up literally in the near future.

Catherine's health improved slightly, then took a turn for the worse, and she decided to have the recommended operation. She continued to suffer much pain. After one bout she whispered, "Don't be alarmed, this is only physical. He has got me! He has got me."

On April 10, 1889, the Salvation Army celebrated William Booth's sixtieth birthday. The Congress Hall was again packed, this time decorated with the banner, *God Bless Our General!* While the Salvationists enjoyed their banquet the Army's "mother," at her own request, lay on a bed in an adjoining room.

After the meal and a speech from the General, Catherine—half-walking, half-carried—entered the hall. For the last time she addressed her faithful people. Unable to stand for more than a brief while, she spoke to them from a chair on the platform.

"Brothers and sisters in Christ, fellow soldiers, as my dear husband was speaking"—her voice was strained but audible—"I was reminded of the bolstering-up, and almost dragging-up, that I sometimes had to do for him in those early days. You would think now that he had always been the bold and (as some people think) self-sufficient man he is, but I can assure you he went forth often with so great trembling and fear for himself that he never would have gone if I had not been behind him!" The crowd laughed at the General's expense. He smiled.

"But I want you now to look at the world in rebellion against God," she continued. "Do not forget the well-to-do people are as much in rebellion against God as the poor. Do not forget that your neighbors and friends, everybody around you, are in rebellion against God. Therefore, whatever hell does mean, whatever your own notions of retribution may be, that retribution is sure to them while they continue in that state of rebellion.

"Look round on them, then buckle to. Be encouraged by what you have heard of what God has done by such feeble instruments, to set yourself to work, to make up your mind as the General did when he was eighteen, that he would spend every bit of his strength, every nerve of his body and all he had in preaching salvation to men. Do that, and then, whether we ever should fight again together or not"—her voice trembled—"we shall meet in the morning."

Few who saw her depart that day had dry eyes, for they knew it would be the last time most of them would see her.

Throughout his wife's long illness Booth agonized over the age-old problem of why one as saintly as his dear Catherine could suffer so terribly. Sometimes he would leave his wife's room and just mutter, "I don't understand it! I don't understand it!" On one occasion he recorded in his diary:

> I am sixty years old, and for the first time, so far as my memory serves me, has God, in infinite mercy, allowed me to have any sorrow that I could not cast upon Him. My mind grows bewildered when I think of the subject, so once more I dismiss it with perhaps the laziest feeling of, "The Lord must do what seemeth good in His sight."

Catherine lingered on for many months, her body in pain, her soul at peace. She was far too sick to attend the twenty-fifth anniversary of the Army in July, but sent a message of greeting to the 50,000 people assembled in the Crystal Palace.

On the first day of October she began to hemorrhage badly, and the family sensed that this was the beginning of the end. She deteriorated rapidly, and two days later, as an evening storm thundered outside, she whispered her farewells to her beloved family.

At one point she cried out, "Now. Yes, Lord, come now!" but the end was not yet.

William sat close to her all night, as she hovered on the brink of eternity. Occasionally she spoke to him in tones too soft for others to hear. He held her hand gently. Morning dawned. She seemed so weak. The end was obviously very near.

Early in the afternoon each member of the family kissed her in turn. She lay there still and silent until at 3:30 she said one word—"Pa." William bent over and kissed her tenderly. She slowly ceased breathing, and entered Glory. The Army Mother had gone to be with her Lord.

34

Darkest England

*T*he month Catherine died William Booth published a book he had written during the heartrending period of his wife's fatal illness. This book, though attacked by many, was to make the Salvation Army what it is today and to gain it the recognition it so justly deserved.

Though Booth's original motivation for beginning his work in the East End of London was purely spiritual, he had grown increasingly concerned about the many social evils that ruined the lives of the people he worked among. The men's homes and the hostels for saved prostitutes had been established because of the poverty and exploitation endured by many people. They were not part of a long-term plan.

They just arose out of necessity.

In Australia, as far back as 1883, Major James Barker had opened his prison-gate home to aid ex-prisoners. It had all been rather haphazard, with no overall plan.

Booth's sighting of those men under London Bridge on a cold winter's night had triggered his sympathies and set his mind working on a plan to launch more social agencies and effectively coordinate them.

He began to formulate his ideas. What were the problems? He listed them, and then outlined each. How could they be solved? That was harder. He labored long to come up with satisfactory solutions. The Gospel had to be at the center of any solution, but there had to be various agencies to help the unemployed, the homeless, and the fallen.

Gradually his jottings came together. Almost without his realizing it, a book was born. As he struggled to complete it, his heart full of grief at his wife's condition, another problem struck him. What should it be called? He needed a title that would capture the nation's imagination. A good title could make the book successful; a bad one would consign it to oblivion.

The explorer Henry Morton Stanley, most famous for finding the long-lost David Livingstone in Africa, had recently published a book. It was the story of his unsuccessful attempt to rescue the governor of Equatoria, Emin Pasha, the victim of a Muslim rebellion. Stanley had led seven hundred men through the dense jungle for over five months in an attempt to pull off the rescue. During the trek, five hundred of his men died. It was a story that captured the hearts of the Victorians, who loved such dramatic adventures. The book was called *In Darkest Africa*.

The story moved Booth. The title had a certain ring about it. Were the denizens of Africa's jungles any worse off than England's slum dwellers? he asked himself. Was there more sin and misery in the tree-rammed jungles of Africa than in the brick and mortar jungles of Britain? Booth found himself answering, "Surely not!" Suddenly the title came to him—*In Darkest England and the Way Out*.

A prior announcement of the book appeared in the *War Cry* of September 20, and exactly a month later it was published.

Its reception surprised everybody. The first edition of 10,000 was sold out within a few days. A hurried reprint of 40,000 hit the bookshops in November, and three further editions were printed the following year.

The book was divided into two parts—*The Darkness*, which outlined the problems, and *Deliverance*, which proposed the remedies.

Why Darkest England? asked the General in the first chapter. He referred to Stanley's book, and the pygmies he had encountered who were unaware of the world of sunshine outside their tree-darkened territory. He likened it to the lot of England's poor. "The lot of a young girl in the Equatorial Forest is not, perhaps, a very happy one, but is it so very much worse than that of many a pretty orphan girl in our Christian capital?"

Booth quoted statistics compiled by his namesake Charles Booth, author of *Life and Labor of the People of London*. These figures estimated that one third of the occupants of London's East

End were at best very poor, and many were starving. William Booth calculated what these figures might mean for the whole country, and concluded that about two million Britons were regularly without sufficient food, and a further million were hardly better off. Thus one tenth of Britain's population, proud owners of an enormous Empire, lived in poverty. The General called them "The Submerged Tenth." Homeless, unemployed, often both, Britain's poor seemed to have no hope.

But Booth believed there was hope. For the pygmies in Africa there was light outside their dark world, though they did not know it. For Booth's "Submerged Tenth" in England he believed there was also light and hope.

His principal recommendations were to set up City Colonies, Farm Colonies, and Colonies Across the Sea, for those in need. He quoted the Salvation Army's experience of ministering to the needs of the destitute and said they had dispensed 3,500,000 meals in just over two years to the needy at low prices. He urged the extension of such work.

But feeding the hungry was not enough, and no one knew that better than Booth. Finding work and permanent shelter were the main needs. He proposed setting up City Industrial Workshops in which the homeless unemployed would be provided with food and a roof over their heads in return for factory-style work. They would also be given financial support and encouragement to find work outside the workshops. When they had achieved that their place would be taken by another in dire need.

In addition, the General proposed to acquire five hundred acres of land on which to locate his first Farm Colony. Having purchased this land he intended to send some of the more able unemployed to the site to organize the colony. Then he would send others from the City Colonies when the work had been established.

Booth anticipated criticism for sending the urban unemployed to work the land. He was bound to be asked, "What do city people know about farming?" But the General had done his homework. "Of sixty cases," he quoted, "examined in the shelters during a fortnight ending on August 2, forty-two were country people." Booth intended returning unemployed countrymen back to gainful employment on the land. More colonies would be established when the first had been stabilized.

When Booth had toured Canada he had noted its vast open spaces and limited population. The thought had germinated and become Colonies Across the Sea. In Canada, the United States, and Australia, there was no shortage of opportunities for those prepared to work. What was needed was a system of supported, mass emigration.

But Booth was not prepared to send just anyone overseas, regardless of credentials. "While men and women would be received into the City Colonies without character," he wrote, "none would be sent overseas who had not been proved worthy of that trust."

That, briefly, was the General's scheme. In anticipation of his readers' question, he asked, "How much will it cost?" He answered, "£1 million to give the scheme a fair chance of getting into practical operation." Booth had set his sights high. £1 million in 1890 was an astronomical sum of money.

Thus Booth presented his plan to the people of Britain. It divided the thinking public.

It was opposed by some noted figures. Professor T. H. Huxley, in correspondence to *The Times* over a two-month period, called it "socialism in disguise." He also asked, "What guarantee is there that thirty years hence the General, who then autocratically controls the actions of, say, 100,000 officers (pledged to blind obedience), will exercise his enormous powers not merely honestly, but wisely?" He also accused Booth of living in luxury, while his officers starved.

C. S. Loch, Secretary of the London Charity Society, believed there was little need for Booth's scheme. He believed the figures the Salvationist quoted were highly questionable.

The Commissioner of London's city police force said Booth's allegations that at times there were over one hundred people sleeping beneath Blackfriars Bridge were "absolutely untrue." His reasoning was that his officers were under instructions not to allow anyone to sleep under the bridges at night, therefore no one did. It did not occur to him that when his men moved a group of the homeless from their bridge shelter they either walked to another bridge or, as soon as the constables had vanished, returned to their haven. The Police Commissioner received full support from London's Lord Mayor, Sir David Bvana. Lord Shaftesbury, son of the renowned reformer, also opposed the *In Darkest England* project.

Some made accusations about Booth's honesty, resurrecting the old rumors that he would abscond with the money. Others alleged that the book was the work of W. T. Stead and not Booth. It is true that Stead had used his journalistic expertise to aid the General in its compilation, but the newspaper man made it clear that the book was written by Booth, not himself. He called the claim "errant nonsense." Still others saw it as a means of tricking people into the Salvation Army's kind of religion.

But there was support, too. One of the main advocates of *In Darkest England* was Archdeacon Farrar of Westminster Abbey. He wrote two letters to the *Daily Graphic* at the turn of the year. He made it clear that in many ways he was critical of Booth and his Army but wrote, "I have never met a scheme that attacks the great problem so fundamentally and so vigorously as that propounded by General Booth." Dr. Farrar, unlike many critics of the plan, took the time and trouble to check the Army's suitability to lead such an undertaking. He was impressed.

Opinion remained divided, particularly on Booth's honesty. Late in 1892 a committee of inquiry was formed to investigate the matter. Their report completely exonerated Booth and his family.

Booth, though it remained unknown to most, had donated the entire profits from the *In Darkest England* book to the project. He did not ask others to do what he was not prepared to do himself.

The press received the report warmly, recognizing that it cleared the General of charges of dishonesty. Even *The Times,* which had been consistently critical of Booth and his soldiers, reluctantly accepted that it cleared Booth's name.

Even in the music halls Booth's victory was celebrated. A song about the plan was written and performed widely. It ran:

Oh, the General's dream,
That Noble Scheme,
Gives John Jones work to do.
He'll have a bed,
And be well fed,
When the General's dreams come true!

The project, meanwhile, had gotten under way as the money became available—even when at times it did not. At one time the social fund was £170,000 in debt, and money was temporarily transferred from general Salvation Army funds to meet the commitments.

Commissioner Elijah Cadman threw himself into the task of supervising the City Colonies with his customary energy. He had by this time learned the rudiments of literacy, but was still far from educated. But what he lacked academically, he made up for in common sense and zeal.

Cadman took over the control of the four men's shelters already functioning and opened another in Southwark Street on the south side of London Bridge, and a sixth in Drury Lane. Additional homes were opened in other cities.

Outside each hostel appeared the bold sign:

NO
homeless or destitute
MAN
who is able and willing to work
NEED
beg, steal, sleep out at night or
COMMIT
SUICIDE
Apply to the officer in charge of this depot

Cadman loved posters!

He also loved men and women. He worked long hours to establish and organize the shelters, with the dedicated support and encouragement of his wife, Maria. Destitute men slept on the primitive, but welcome beds. Food was dispensed at a minimum price. No one had to stay. Salvation Army homes, unglamorous though they were, were infinitely preferable to the workhouses.

Elijah Cadman persevered with the task for most of that decade. There were times when he would have loved to have been given another job, but International Headquarters decreed that he should continue with it, and continue with it he did.

The second part of the scheme started in March 1891, when a deposit was paid on eight hundred acres of land near Southend in Essex. On the border of the land Booth, who liked signs almost as much as Cadman, had erected a notice which read:

The Salvation Army
Darkest England
The Castle and Park Farms with other properties
have been purchased by General Booth for the
establishment of the first Farm Colony and
elimination of the Submerged Tenth.

In May a small group of men were sent to prepare the site for use. They erected buildings for accommodation, a small hospital, and a mission hall.

The project became a reality in October when over two hundred men joined the pioneers and began farming the precious piece of real estate. No farm is established overnight, but the men had a job to do, a roof over their heads and provisions. For the most part they were content.

In 1893 the president of the Board of Agriculture visited Hadleigh Farm Colony, as it had been named. He was impressed and promised to investigate the possibility of acquiring government funds to extend the work. The Colony was extended to over 3,000 acres a few years later, partly with government money.

Two years later Cecil Rhodes, on a brief trip to England, was impressed by what he saw at Hadleigh. By then the Colony operated a market garden, orchards, a flock of sheep, a herd of Lincoln Shorthorns, and a herd of pigs. It also had a brick works.

The overseas colonies never came into being. It was the only major part of Booth's plan that was not set in motion. Australian and New Zealand authorities would not cooperate with the Army on this matter. They saw it as Britain disposing of their less desirable, even criminal, elements to other lands.

That and other difficulties proved insurmountable, and the idea was finally abandoned in 1910. Salvationists in other lands, however, did set up their own Farm Colonies, most notably in Rhodesia, Holland, and America.

Bramwell came up with a satisfactory variant of the Colonies Across the Sea—an emigration program. In the early 1890s a small trickle of Salvation Army-aided emigrants began to depart Britain's shores, mainly for North America. Ten years later men were leaving Hadleigh a hundred at a time to go to Canada. Later still, the Army chartered several ships to increase the flow of emigrants.

PART III

THE WORLD

35

Persecution in Switzerland

The Salvation Army had become a worldwide organization by the turn of the century, with soldiers in every continent. In Europe the Army was fighting in France, Switzerland, Holland, Belgium, Germany, Denmark, Norway, Finland, Sweden, and Spain. In the Americas, apart from the United States, it was established in Canada, Jamaica, Barbados, Argentina, and Uruguay. Asia had Salvationists in Indonesia, Japan, and Hong Kong as well as in India. In Africa, Rhodesia, South Africa, and Zululand were under attack by God's Army, and New Zealand had joined Australia as the earliest of the South Pacific countries to see the Army commence its work.

Nowhere was the Salvation Army more severely repulsed than in Switzerland. To launch the attack there the General chose twenty-six-year-old Arthur Clibborn. Clibborn had been brought up as a Quaker in County Armagh in Ireland, joined the Salvation Army and quickly rose to the rank of Colonel. He had previously served with "La Marechale" in France and spoke French fluently.

At the end of 1882 he held his first meeting in Geneva. Most of his congregation were quite different from those who normally frequented Army mission halls and, like the Athenians listening to Paul on Mars Hill, were there largely out of intellectual curiosity. The meeting achieved nothing.

Clibborn was a very able organizer but not a good speaker, so Booth decided to transfer his eldest daughter and some French officers from France to Switzerland to put some fire into the campaign. The fire materialized, and it came from both sides in the war.

The traditionally peace-loving Swiss, with their Calvinistic heritage, found this military style of Armenian Christianity hard to accept. La Marechale began what was intended to be a series of meetings in the Casino Hall at Christmastime. The opposition from the beginning was intense. As the Salvationists sang hymns, their congregation sang rude songs. When Katie Booth prayed, such was the uproar that nobody could hear her. At the end of the meeting a mob of students followed the Salvationists home, taunting and threatening.

A second meeting was held with the same results, and the manager of the Casino Hall told them that they could not use the building again. They then moved to the Reformation Hall, where the same pattern of unruly behavior occurred. On their way back to their quarters La Marechale and her colleagues were pelted with stones and pieces of wood. So menacing was the manner of the crowd that Katie Booth asked for police protection. The authorities not only failed to provide it, but made it clear that the Salvation Army was not wanted in Switzerland.

At the beginning of February a decree was passed by which Salvation Army services were banned throughout Geneva. But the move so disturbed some of the Swiss people that a protest was sent to the government signed by over nine hundred people. It said the trouble at Salvation Army meetings could have been controlled if the police had been used. It also pointed out that two federal rights had been violated by the Canton's decree—the liberty of the individual and freedom of religion. But the petition failed.

The situation worsened. The Salvation Army Swiss headquarters and the homes of known Salvationist sympathizers came under attack. Stones and bottles were hurled through their windows, so that to remain in the buildings was dangerous. But to venture outside was even more so. Anyone who dared leave the headquarters was beaten by the waiting mob, even though police were present. They just watched and laughed.

Two of the Canton's newspapers strongly criticized this new religion and encouraged the activities of their tormentors.

On February 8, Katie Booth was summoned to police headquarters and interviewed at great length. Four days later she was expelled from Geneva, and left the work there in the hands of two French officers and the converts they had made amidst the furor.

A fighter by nature, the eldest of Booth's daughters went to the nation's capital, Berne, where Clibborn was already appealing to the President. The appeal failed. Not only was the Salvation Army considered too noisy and disruptive, but women preaching in a public place could not be tolerated.

They continued their preaching in the face of continual opposition, official and otherwise. Like the early disciples, as they were expelled from one town they went to another, taking the Good News. They refused to be silenced.

Their first convert in Geneva had been a youth called Charles Wyssa. Shortly after joining the Army, Wyssa was attacked and severely beaten by his workmates. He never fully recovered from that act of violence, and soon after he caught tuberculosis and died. Katie Booth heard of his death while in jail in Neuchatel. She requested bail that she might go to the young man's funeral. To her surprise it was granted, and she attended the funeral, conducted in the garden of his family's home.

The service was led by Clibborn and, apart from the family and numerous Salvationists, Josephine Butler, who happened to be lecturing in Switzerland, was present. It was a beautiful, warm autumn day. The breeze rustled the leaves of the trees, and the birds joined in joyful harmony with the group as they sang their songs. The mourners stood around the coffin, which was placed upon a table in the garden.

As the service went on, the Chief of Police, who had been observing events flanked by a dozen officers, walked toward the Salvationists who by then stood with heads bowed in prayer.

"This assembly is illegal," he said. "You must disperse immediately."

The ceremony continued. No one opened an eye. No one showed any sign of having heard him.

He repeated his demand in a louder, more aggressive tone. Still no one reacted. Frustrated he moved smartly toward La

Marechale and grabbed her by the arm. "You are under arrest," he said.

She angrily shook off his hand, turned to him and said in a fierce whisper, "May I remind you that you are in the presence of the dead. Show some respect. If you wish to speak to me, it must wait until after this service."

The Chief recoiled at her fiery expression, and retreated to where his officers awaited him, his face red with anger. Looking back he mumbled, "We'll call in the troops if you don't stop this nonsense." He then led his constables away, and the service continued.

All the undertakers who had been asked to take care of the burial arrangements had refused to have anything to do with the burial of a Salvationist. So when the service had ended six of the group hoisted the coffin onto their shoulders and led the solemn but proud procession to the cemetery, singing hymns. On the way, one lone constable ordered them to stop singing. They complied with the request.

After Wyssa had been laid in the ground, the Chief of Police returned with the mayor and approached Katie.

"You are under arrest," snapped the Chief.

She looked at both men with a defiant glare. "You may not know, gentlemen, but I am on bail from the prison in Neuchatel. You might advise me how I can go to two different prisons in two different cities at one time," she said forcefully.

The two officials opened their mouths in stunned silence, and looked questioningly at each other.

La Marechale went on, "May I go to Neuchatel, or do you wish me to accept your hospitality here in Geneva?"

Again, the two men looked at each other in confusion. Finally the mayor spoke. "You may go to Neuchatel, but you must leave immediately."

Katie Booth left the cemetery straightaway, and Geneva within the hour. Unknown to her one of her soldiers was later arrested for saying "Amen!" too loudly, and later still Clibborn was expelled from Geneva.

Upon returning to Neuchatel, La Marechale was imprisoned for twelve days awaiting trial. She was eventually tried along with a French-speaking officer from the Channel Islands, Captain Edward Becquet, who had previously worked with her in Paris. The trial started on September 27, and it was not until October 1 that the jury went to consider their verdict. After several hours of deliberation, they filed back into the packed courtroom. The judge questioned them about their decision.

"Did the accused take part in a meeting?" he asked.

"Yes," replied the foreman.

"Was the meeting in violation of the decree?"

"Yes," again came the reply.

"Have they acted with culpable intentions?"

A long pause followed the third question. The court was hushed. Then, "No," came the reply. A gasp went up from the crowd.

"In consequence of this verdict the accused are acquitted," pronounced the judge.

The court erupted with shouts of "Hallelujah!" and "Praise the Lord!" from the joyous Salvation soldiers. As the victors left the court, they became aware that all the police, who had been present in substantial numbers inside and outside the court during the trial, had vanished. Surrounding the court, unrestrained, was the mob.

La Marechale, Becquet, and their supporters looked at the angry throng. They glanced at one another, nervously. "Well, brothers and sisters," said their leader, "we can't go back into the court and we can't stay here on the steps, so there is only one way for us, and that is straight ahead. May God protect us."

She began to walk slowly but decisively down the steps. Her soldiers followed in the direction of the screaming rabble. They pushed their way into the mob, who started to kick, punch, and spit on them. Bonnets and caps were thrown to the ground and trampled underfoot. Uniforms were soiled and torn. But they continued to push their way through the crowd. The journey home was slow and painful, and they arrived at their destinations bruised and sore, but triumphant. Katie Booth's prayer had been answered.

36

Mixed Blessings in the United States and Canada

*T*he first meeting held in Canada under the Salvation Army flag was, appropriately, in London, Ontario in 1882. It was conducted in the open air by two Salvationists from England, Jack Addie and Joe Ludgate.

In Canada public support for the Army was almost immediate, though officialdom frowned upon it. The London City Council passed an ordinance that forbade open-air meetings and the beating of drums in public places, specifically to silence the Army. Jack Addie did not wish to break the law, but he felt he had no alternative. So he continued to preach out-of-doors, as had been his habit. A large crowd gathered to hear him. It was so sympathetic to Addie and antagonistic to the police that the constables dared not arrest him in public. Instead they visited his home that night, informing him that he must appear in court the next day.

The following morning he went to court, was fined $5 or ten days jail, but by some now-forgotten circumstance suffered neither.

Later Captain Anna Shirley was sent to London to lead the troops converted through Addie and Ludgate, and Captain Charles Wass was sent to Toronto from New York to establish the work there. The Canadian Forces at that time came under American command.

In 1884 Canada became a separate territory led by Major Thomas Coombs. By then there were more than forty corps, and about one hundred officers throughout the country. Eight years later Herbert Booth became Commander of the Canadian Territory. He inherited a divided Army. When he arrived on the scene he found a considerable body of officers, under the leadership of Brigadier Peter Philpott, on the point of resigning because of what they considered unfair treatment.

He mediated between the feuding factions and gained a fragile peace. The ill feeling continued for a couple of years, and eventually Philpott, with a few other officers, did leave the Army.

Staff-Captain William McIntyre, in Newfoundland, which was then an independent island off Canada's east coast, initiated an entirely new venture—a Salvation Navy.

McIntyre, a tireless visitor of people near and far, found himself inconveniently dependent upon the whims and times of various boats when visiting his scattered troops, most of whom were inaccessible by land. How could he visit when he liked and as often as he liked? The answer came in the little vessel, *The Glad Tidings*. The craft went to Newfoundland's numerous harbors, taking the Good News to people with little or no other opportunity to hear it. William McIntyre, who had left home in his early teens and had become a Salvationist soon after, was an innovator.

———

In the United States, the Army continued to grow, under Ballington Booth's command. When George Railton visited America in 1893 to speak at a congress in New York, he found the organization far larger and healthier than he had dared expect when he pioneered the venture thirteen years before. He spoke at a crowded Carnegie Hall to 5,000 men and women on two successive nights. Many more were unable to enter the packed building.

Railton was delighted with such a show of strength. The atmosphere of the meetings was electric, and the Commissioner called the congress "one of the most devil-defying and God-glorifying exhibitions of the power of Christ in human hearts and lives ever displayed in this world."

The Army had spread to most states in the eastern half of the country. Its influence affected spheres far beyond the purely religious and, though sometimes that made it enemies, it also made the Army many friends.

The role of the church at times of industrial strife has always been difficult. In 1894 at Fall River in Massachusetts, the workers at the textile mill went on strike for three months.

With only meager resources to fall back upon, many of the strikers were reduced to destitution, but still held out. Whole families were on the point of starvation, and many Salvationists were among them.

The local Captain, Alexander "Jimmy" Lamb, was a worried, saddened man as he saw children begging in the streets, but was unable to meet their need. As the situation worsened a businessman offered to donate $25 of food daily, if someone would volunteer to prepare meals for the hungry. Lamb wasted no time. He contacted the man, organized his out-of-work soldiers, and they turned their barracks into a dining room. Each day over five hundred tasted the Army's hospitality, and the donor's generosity carried them through until the crisis was over.

George Pullman, originator of the sleeping-car on the railways, ran his business in a ruthless manner. He not only owned the business, but also the homes in which his employees lived in the Illinois township. When he cut their wages and increased their rents, 3,000 angry workers came out on strike.

Pullman, who refused to recognize trade unions, would not relent. The workers were determined to make him. The industrial strife escalated until at one time there were about 100,000 railwaymen out on strike.

After two months the original strikers were in dire straits. But as the news of the seriousness of their plight reached Chicago, Salvationist Captain Wallace Winchell took action. He visited Governor Peter Altgeld with a plan, which gained the politician's approval.

He then proceeded to saturate the "Windy City" with leaflets and posters requesting food and clothing for the strikers. The response was overwhelming. Cash as well as food and clothing were received in great quantities, and Winchell led the resulting wagon train of supplies to the unfortunate town.

The Booth family was full of fiery individuals. They worked together, but tensions were often evident. Until her death in 1890, Catherine had been the adhesive that held the family together. When she was "promoted to glory" the family began to divide. What Catherine had been able to do, William Booth could not.

A little over five years after Catherine's death, Ballington and Maud Booth, the American Commanders, resigned from the Salvation Army. Ballington explained the reasons for their stand in a long letter to Bramwell. The crux of it was that he, and some other American officers, objected to taking orders from a Chief-of-Staff in another land who knew little of the different circumstances in the United States and frequently made decisions affecting them without consultation.

What probably rankled most of all was Bramwell's order for the Ballington Booths to leave America to take on another command. Nearly twenty years before, Bramwell and Railton had delighted to be under the authority of William Booth, but Ballington had no longer any intention of taking orders from his older brother.

Bramwell's reply ran to 8,000 words. In it he urged, "Ballington, do not do it! As you value your own soul and the peace of your conscience, and the happiness of Maud and your children, I say again from my deepest heart, do not do it!"

The General was in India when the bombshell struck, but Bramwell sent him a telegram advising him of the defection.

He wrote to his son, "Oh, Ballington, Ballington! You cannot be in your right reason. The whole thing is like a horrid dream. For your own sake hesitate! Think! Return! The worst can yet be averted. The past may be forgiven. Believe me to be still your affectionate father. Praying for you all the time."

But Ballington's mind was made up. What remained was to discover whether the other leaders of the American Salvation Army felt the same way as he. He called a meeting at the American Headquarters, now in New York, and behind locked doors presented to them the reasons for his resignation.

Eva Booth, who was working in New York at the time of Ballington's resignation, had been given temporary command of the American territory, but found herself locked out of the meeting. Her concern over what was going on inside the building made her determined to gain entry. So she walked from the Fourteenth Street main entrance into Thirteenth Street, went up the fire escape and climbed in through a window, despite the inconvenience of her long skirts. She made her way to the meeting hall and mounted the platform. The assembly gasped at her unexpected appearance, and then went silent. Her red hair curled vividly beneath her bonnet, as she fixed her piercing eyes upon her surprised brother.

"I wish to speak, Ballington," she said firmly.

Ballington hesitated as he looked his sister in the eye. He knew that letting her speak could lose him the day, but to defy her, he knew from childhood, was ill-advised. "You may," he consented.

He then turned to the gathering and said, "Commissioner Eva Booth will now address us."

Of all the orators in the Booth family, it was Eva who ranked second to her father. Her speech was fiery, her words persuasive. She did not denounce her brother, but made it clear that for them to resign en masse from the Salvation Army would be a disaster—not just for that Army, but for the church of Jesus Christ. It would be an act of treason not just to the General, but to the Lord. Ballington had been out-maneuvered. His sister had the rapt attention of his congregation.

Following the meeting, the majority of American Salvationists remained loyal to William Booth. A few joined Ballington and Maud in their breakaway organization, which was to be named the Volunteers of America. Ballington became the second member of the Booth family to become a General. His followers elected him to that rank for a term of five years.

The new Commanders of the American Salvation Army were Frederick and Emma Booth-Tucker, who had recently arrived back in England from India.

They set out from England, obedient to their orders, leaving behind their sick infant son. As the pilot was about to leave the ship they were on, they received the message that the little boy, Tancred, had not long to live. The ship's captain refused to allow Emma to descend into the pilot's vessel, which was being tossed about in a rough sea, so instead Frederick went back to England to be at his son's side.

Tancred showed very positive signs of recovery after his father's return, so Frederick embarked on the next ship due for New York. Three days later Tancred died. Neither of his parents knew until they reached America.

Early in 1898 the General made another tour of America, during which he received the honor of being asked to open the American Senate in prayer. Booth was more readily accepted by

America's leaders than by his own nation's.

The work of the Booth-Tuckers in America was highly successful. Determined to save those most in need, Frederick often donned shabby clothes and went about the slums taking the Gospel to the poor. So wholeheartedly did he play the part that on one occasion he was arrested for vagrancy. Frederick and Emma, with patience and hard work, successfully healed most of the wounds left by the secession of Ballington and Maud Booth.

It was a sad loss when Emma and Colonel Holland were killed in a train crash when visiting forces in Chicago.

Frederick Booth-Tucker continued as Commander in America until replaced by his dynamic sister-in-law, Eva (by then named Evangeline) Booth, in 1904.

Evangeline was an entertainer in a church of performers. In one town she was billed as:

> MISS BOOTH IN RAGS
> Will tell the tale
> of a broken heart
> and sing the song of love.

If she had to don rags to win souls, then she would do so. If the requirement was standing on her head, then she would do that. On this occasion she turned up in tatters and held a 4,000-strong audience captivated as she told them of her work among the poor in the East End of London. But *her* aim was not to entertain. She desired to bring men and women to Christ. She reasoned that people were more likely to listen to and accept the Gospel if it was presented in a way that held their attention.

Commander Evangeline Booth was not the only member of the American forces unafraid to use sensational methods to present the Gospel. Colonel William McIntyre was also prepared to try anything. Impressed by the testimonies of numerous converted drunks that he had heard in New York, the idea came to him of rounding up as many drunks as possible and, using some of the more remarkable converts, presenting Christ to them.

On November 25, 1909, (Thanksgiving Day) the project was launched, and named "Boozer's Day." Buses were hired and driven around the streets before dawn to pick up the alcoholics sleeping off the previous night's binge in doorways and down side streets.

The first group were left at the Memorial Hall in Fourteenth Street, then the buses drove away again to collect more. News traveled. The press arrived. What a story! The Memorial Hall was rapidly filling up with a dirty, smelly influx of drunken humanity. Eventually well over 1,000 inebriates filled the hall. Liberal doses of coffee were dispensed in an attempt to sober up as many as possible so that they could understand the Gospel.

One ex-drunkard, a sailor, stood up to address the noisy throng. "I used to drink like a fish," he claimed, "but now if the whole Atlantic were whisky, and I got dumped overboard, having to spend the rest of my life swimming around in it, I wouldn't open my gills for a drop!"

Other men and women stood up to testify. In between times music was played by the big band that had been assembled.

During the day, McIntyre received a note from one of the men. It read, "I am a hopeless drunk. I can't cure myself. I am going to commit suicide." The Colonel invited the man up onto the platform, where he coaxed the man to slowly tell him his story in private.

When he had finished McIntyre spoke to the crowd. "This man thinks he is past hope," shouted the Colonel.

"Never!" came a call from the body of the hall.

"All can be saved!" yelled a woman.

"He wants to commit suicide. Would you like this man to kill himself, or be converted and become a new creature in Christ?" asked McIntyre.

"A new creature!" came a voice.

"Convert 'im, Colonel!" shouted another.

Cheers arose from around the hall, and calls of "Amen!"

"My dear man," said McIntyre, turning to the drunk, "there is hope. You are not beyond the reach of the Lord Jesus Christ. I will take you to the penitent bench, and one of my officers will help you." So the Colonel took the man by the arm, and led him down the platform stairs. That day the would-be suicide was one of over two hundred who expressed faith in Christ.

Commander Evangeline Booth applauded such ingenious, aggressive Christianity, and so did the General.

37

The Battle of
"The Meadow of Happiness"

Shinobu Nagasaka had been brought up as a Buddhist in Japan. He and his wife became Christians and went to live for a while in America. When in San Francisco they encountered the Salvation Army. They were so impressed that they went to London in 1893 to meet William Booth, with the intention of setting up the Army in their native land.

It was not until two years later that Colonel and Mrs. Edward Wright, who had pioneered the work in Brisbane, set sail for Japan. By the time they arrived in Yokohama they had acquired Japanese clothing, and disembarked with the intention of living like the natives.

When Edward was walking through the European section of the town just two days after their arrival, he heard a piano being played and a man singing:

The Salvation Army has come!
The Salvation Army has come!
O Lord have mercy upon us!
The Salvation Army has come!

The Wrights knew they would not get any sympathy from their fellow countrymen.

They set up their headquarters in Tokyo, calling themselves *Kyu Sei Gun* (Save the World Army). The first meeting was held in the YMCA Hall, which was packed.

One Japanese property owner was so impressed with what

he saw and heard that he told Wright that he would order all his tenants to join the Army. If they refused he would evict them. When Wright explained that that was not right, that people could not become Christians by force, the man relented. Instead, he told Wright, he would only raise the rents of those who refused to join. Further protest, through an interpreter, proved useless, and there the matter remained.

One young Japanese Christian, Gunpei Yamamuro, made contact with the Salvation Army to size it up and see if its people were genuine. He had previously been a Christian pastor, but had resigned to join the secular workforce so that he might have contact with as many non-Christians as possible, such was his burden for souls. Yamamuro was deeply impressed by everything he saw, heard, and read. He joined the Army and quickly became a lieutenant, the first Japanese-born Salvation Army officer.

After the work had become established in Japan, Colonel Henry Bullard was transferred from India to replace Wright. One day Bullard and Yamamuro witnessed a colorful procession making its way through Tokyo's streets. Carriages, gaily decorated with flowers, were followed by dozens of attractive young women in beautiful highly colored silk kimonos. Even though the parade was so bright and picturesque, it had a strange, almost mournful feel about it which perplexed Bullard.

When the rear of the procession was disappearing in the distance, the Englishman turned to his companion and asked, "Who were they, Gunpei?"

The Japanese looked Bullard in the eye, and said, "That, my dear friend, was the Feast of the Lanterns procession. It is held every year. They were all prostitutes."

"Prostitutes? Prostitutes? That many? And so public?" exclaimed the shocked Colonel.

"That is only some of them," answered Yamamuro. "They come from the *Yoshiwara,* or Meadow of Happiness. But what goes on there is anything but happy. It is said that there are five thousand girls there, in what is almost a city within a city."

"Five thousand!" Bullard's voice was incredulous.

"Yes, and many of them are held against their will. Some have been given by their families as a guarantee against a loan granted during times of hardship," said the Lieutenant.

Bullard was stunned. He collected his thoughts. "Why is it allowed? Is it legal?" he asked.

"Not really!" came the answer. "At least, not their being held against their will. I think the law says that no one can be held against a debt, too. But if so, it is never enforced."

"We can't let this go on, Gunpei. We must do something," stated Bullard.

"But what?" asked Yamamuro.

"Let's check on the law first. How can we do that?" questioned the Colonel.

"I have a friend who might be able to help us," replied the Japanese.

So they visited Yamamuro's friend Ibara Kondo, who confirmed that it was illegal to hold a person against his will in lieu of debt. The law at least was on their side.

"Indeed," said Kondo, "earlier this year, an American missionary in Nagoya—Murphy, I think his name was—won a court case on behalf of two girls who had run away from a brothel."

"We ought to make contact with this Mr. Murphy," said Bullard, turning to his companion. "Would that be possible, do you think?"

"I will make enquiries, Colonel," replied Yamamuro.

"I think I might be able to find his address for you," offered Kondo.

Having obtained the address, Bullard wrote to Murphy, requesting advice on how to tackle the problem. Murphy's reply, with further help from Kondo, was a firm base on which to build their campaign.

The main problem was ignorance of the law. The law was written in classical Japanese, which was understood by very few. Yamamuro therefore had the relevant part translated into contemporary Japanese, and Bullard printed a special edition of the Japanese *War Cry—Toki-no-Koe*—with the translation on the front page. An open letter to the prostitutes accompanied it. It read:

"As I think of your misfortune, I cannot keep silent. You are like birds in a cage, your bodies seduced by drunkards, liars and thieves. You must resolve to give up this way of life. No living person, no matter how heavy his debt, can be forced to do painful service against his will. Contact us—we are prepared to take care of you."

The two officers were under no illusion about what could

happen to them once the paper began to reach its targets. The men who ran Yoshiwara would fight back, and their methods would not be gentlemanly.

That night they called together as many of their flock as they could contact and then spent the night in prayer.

In the morning about fifty Salvationists, led by Bullard playing his cornet, Yamamuro, and Major Charles Duce, marched on Yoshiwara. They launched their attack upon an unprepared enemy. The Japanese-speaking officers shouted aloud their cause. As women came from the buildings they were given copies of *Toki-no-Koe*.

They were invited by the Salvationists to accompany them to the Rescue Home which had already been prepared for them. The women gathered around excitedly in a swirl of colored silk, taking the papers and reading them.

The devil's armies are never slow to retaliate, and in spite of the surprise of the attack the brothel-keepers quickly caught on to what was happening. Gradually a host of men emerged from all directions, many armed with staves. The prostitutes vanished noisily and quickly as they saw their owners, aware of their masters' anger.

The Salvationists were surrounded and outnumbered. A volley of stones cascaded into them as they stood nervously pondering their next move. Then, with a fearful scream, the mob attacked, sticks flailing, at the hapless Christians. As one Salvationist avoided an aggressor, he ran into another and was beaten to the ground. Bullard's cornet was wrenched from his hands and trampled on as he was beaten by two of the thugs. All around, Bullard's men and women were being struck and knocked to the ground.

Suddenly the police arrived and the assailants retreated, to the relief of the Christians. There was scarcely one of the party unbloodied, but miraculously none were seriously hurt, and they slowly wended their way back to the hall.

Later their headquarters was the scene of an invasion—an invasion by journalists. For the first time they showed an interest in this strange religious organization. Next day all the newspapers came down on the side of the Salvation Army.

But press support and continued police protection were not enough. Even though the senior Salvation Army officers were shadowed by the police for months after the initial attack, Charles Duce was captured by the irate brothel-keepers and nearly beaten to death. The office of two of the newspapers also came under attack and had their equipment destroyed. But the press continued to support the Army.

Eventually the Mikado issued an Imperial Ordinance which stated that any girl who wished to leave Yoshiwara could do so, and anyone who attempted to stop a prostitute leaving would face legal action. It was then that Bullard put the second part of their plan into operation, and thousands of leaflets were distributed, urging the girls to give up prostitution and report to the Rescue Home. The brothel-keepers, now thoroughly defeated, went around buying the leaflets at ten yen each in a vain attempt to stop them from falling into the hands of their girls.

It is estimated that in the two years after the first march on Yoshiwara about fourteen thousand prostitutes left their profession. Some of them became Salvationists.

Nearly twenty years later Bullard and Duce were two of only five Europeans listed in a Benefactors of Japan roll.

Meanwhile, as the nineteenth century came to a close, Commissioner James Dowdle had repeated bouts of sickness. He had served in several countries, often accompanying the General on his overseas tours. He had labored for long hours, and the strain had taken its toll.

The Hallelujah Fiddle was heard less often, and when it was it seemed to lack its old sparkle. When well enough the Commissioner still preached, but Dowdle knew he was dying. He realized that soon he would go to meet his Lord.

On July 21, 1900, the Hallelujah Fiddle finally fell silent. James Dowdle had died. His effervescent, exuberant spirit had gone to be with his God.

38

Defections

*B*ramwell, unlike the other members of the Booth family, was deskbound. As Chief-of-Staff his role was almost entirely administrative. His main task was the dispatching of staff to the various parts of the battlefield, like a chess grand master playing ten games at once. He fulfilled his task with great dedication, at times wishing that he could join his brethren on the front line. But if duty to God and obedience to his General meant spending most of his time at International Headquarters, then he would do that.

His decisions were not always popular, particularly within the family. Where his brothers and sisters were prepared to obey the General, they were not as ready to sit under his authority. His deteriorating hearing tended to isolate him from his colleagues.

Catherine (La Marechale) Booth had married Arthur Clibborn in February 1887, and they took the surname Booth-Clibborn. They worked in various European countries after their marriage, including France, Belgium, and Holland.

As 1901 drew to its conclusion, Arthur became more and more fascinated by a sect called The Zion Movement. His wife became more and more dissatisfied with the government of the Salvation Army.

The leader of The Zion Movement was a charismatic figure called Dr. John Alexander Dowie, who claimed to be the prophet Elijah heralding the Second Coming of Christ. Booth-Clibborn was impressed. At the end of November he wrote to Dowie: "I have decided to offer myself to you, dear doctor, and do so, firmly believing it to be the will of God." His wife was not in agreement

162

with his views on Dowie, but because of her discontent with her father's Army and faithfulness to her marriage vows, she knew that she must resign too.

Bramwell, on hearing of their intention to leave the Army, contacted them in haste to try to persuade them to change their minds. But their minds were made up, and in January 1902 the Booth-Clibborns officially resigned.

Herbert Booth, like Ballington before him, had crossed swords with Bramwell. He had asked for and moved the Australian command almost, it seemed, with a view to getting as far away from Bramwell as possible. His dissatisfaction went back as far as 1897, and over a period of nearly five years it had developed dramatically. While in charge of the Australian troops he increasingly expressed a desire for a change in the Army's administration. Like Ballington, he felt that each country should have almost total independence from International Headquarters. Bramwell did not.

Two weeks after the Booth-Clibborns resigned, Herbert and his wife, Corrie, followed suit. Their letter of resignation read in part:

> "Our Dear Father and General, to us, and to you, the contents of this letter are of a supremely melancholy nature. Judge of the greater agony it has given us to write it by the pain it will cause you to read it.
>
> "We find ourselves in a condition absolutely without heart to face any further responsibilities under the direction of International Headquarters. We must sorrowfully admit that the present method of Army administration will no longer commend itself to our judgments nor is it in harmony with the dictates of our conscience.
>
> "The system which subjugates all the chief officers of the Army to the vote of their subordinates and yet leaves the supreme heads in absolute control seems to us unjust, unreasonable, and oppressive."

Two double resignations within his own family so close together had saddened, but not destroyed the old General. He was hurt but not defeated. He was strong-willed, and so were most of his family. Sometimes those wills clashed, but the central matter to Booth was not his family, but his Army, his precious Army.

Shortly after those departures, Booth was again touring

America. At one appointment he made his feelings on the subject plain. He said, "My blessed children have helped me. It is true that one or two have fallen from my side, but I love them, and they have fallen to come back again sooner or later. I say my children have helped me; but the Salvation Army does not belong to the Booth family. It belonged to the Salvation Army. So long as the Booth family are good Salvationists and worthy of commands, they shall have them, but only if they are. I am not the General of a family. I am the General of the Salvation Army, and when the flag falls from my grasp I will do my best to ensure another takes it up who shall be better than the old General, as the new and young are believed to be better than the old."

The General was by then seventy-three years of age. He still ploughed through a remarkable amount of work, showing little signs of slowing down, but he knew that his "promotion to Glory" might not be far away. Thoughts about his successor as General, which was his decision and his alone, had long been in his mind. A little while after his wife's death he had decided to commit his choice to paper. The name of that successor was then locked away in the safe of the Army's lawyer Dr. Alfred Ranger. No one but William Booth and Ranger knew who had been chosen.

39

In the United States Again

*F*or much of the remainder of the General's life he traveled throughout Britain and overseas, preaching, encouraging, and meeting the lowly and the great.

He set out on another trip to America on the *SS Philadelphia*.

His reception in New York was tumultuous. As the ship arrived in the early hours of the morning, most passengers, including the General and his aide, John Lawley, remained aboard asleep. The slumbers of even the most fatigued were, however, rudely interrupted at dawn.

BOOM! BOOM! BOOM!

Passengers, wiping the sleep from their eyes, peered through the portals and rushed to the decks to discover the cause of the explosions. The Salvation Army was welcoming its General. A flotilla of gaily decorated craft had come alongside the *Philadelphia*, and one enthusiastic Salvationist was giving his leader a salute from an old cannon.

Hundreds of flag-waving Salvationists were crowded on the various boats cheering their General, who had just become visible on the ship's deck. He waved back. John Lawley stood by his side, smiling broadly.

A band on one of the vessels began playing, and the music of familiar hymns and Army songs wafted over the harbor. Frederick Booth-Tucker came on board the *Philadelphia* to welcome his General and escort him off the ship.

Upon disembarking, Booth was taken to the American Headquarters, and later presented to the people of New York City by its mayor, Mr. Seth Low, at a special dinner. At the dinner Booth leaned over to Lawley and said, "All this for us, Commissioner! Just over twenty years ago we were banned from preaching in the streets in New York—now they treat us like celebrities."

"God is good, General," responded Lawley. "He has certainly overcome prejudice against us in this place."

After the meal the mayor stood to make his official speech of welcome. He began with the customary formalities, then went on to tell of an encounter he had had with a clergyman a few years before. "I asked this dear man," said the mayor, "what he thought of the Salvation Army. He replied, 'To tell you the truth, I don't like it at all. But to be candid with you, I believe that God Almighty does.'"

The audience laughed its approval. Booth beamed in satisfaction.

From New York, Booth traveled into Canada, conducting crusades in Toronto and Winnipeg, and holding single meetings in smaller towns. Traveling south, he crossed the border, again, going to Chicago, Kansas City, far west to San Francisco, and then southeast to New Orleans and on to Tennessee.

His first official engagement in Washington was at a dinner with fifty prominent politicians and businessmen, arranged by Senator Mark Hanna.

The night was cold—the atmosphere in the dining room was scarcely less so. Most of the guests had come to see a curiosity, a freak. Booth sensed it. There was little conversation during the meal, which seemed to last forever. The General was uncomfortable. He felt fifty pairs of eyes trained on him.

At the end of the meal Hanna rose to introduce the General. As the Senator finished, a ripple of polite applause broke out around the dining room.

William Booth stood up. He had spoken thousands of times before in public, on nearly two hundred occasions on this present tour, but never had he felt so embarrassed, so lost for words. He would have gladly swapped this small group of well-to-dos for any number of raving drunks. But there was no escape. He began in a hoarse whisper. His voice had suffered over the non-stop speaking engagements of the previous three months. Only half of the gathering could hear him.

"Louder!" demanded a senator most distant from him.

Hanna looked down at the table. *Have I made a mistake?* he

thought. *Surely this man Booth can do better than this.*

But the shout had brought Booth to his senses. Were politicians and millionaires so very different from prostitutes and thieves? Were they not all sinners? He would apeak boldly on what he knew best, Christ's Gospel and the Salvation Army.

"Oh! I can shout if necessary," he responded to the senator, in a voice clearly audible to all, "and what I have to say should be shouted—shouted from the housetops.

"As I have visited the towns and cities throughout your great country, I have seen all kinds of sin and degradation. I have seen sinners in the poorer sections of the community, and I have seen them, too, in the wealthier, more favored segments of society. But sin is not the monopoly of the poor, nor the rich. It is common to man." Booth was now in his stride, almost, but not quite, forgetting the nature of his audience. Hanna was also feeling more comfortable.

"I have seen many of my officers laboring among drunks and prostitutes, thieves and the unemployed, frequently with much interference from officialdom," Booth continued. Now some of the other diners were feeling a shade uncomfortable.

"On other occasions, though less often, we have received support from those who rule. America is a Christian country. Many of you are Christians. We need your support. We fight for Jesus Christ against sin. We battle against society's evils. We do not want your opposition. We want your recognition that what we do is for the benefit of your people." The General now felt relaxed. His words were delivered with emotion. His arms spread wide to embrace the nation. He thumped the table to emphasize a point, imperiling the coffee cups. The icy atmosphere in the room had melted.

Booth spoke for an hour. He addressed the men to whom the spoken word was their stock in trade, yet the change in their attitude to him was obvious well before he had finished.

"Gentlemen," he concluded, aware that he had won his audience, "the hope of America is Jesus Christ. The Salvation Army unashamedly preaches Jesus Christ. We reach those whom the churches normally do not contact. America needs the Salvation Army."

As Booth sat down, silence greeted him, yet that silence did not feel antagonistic. Slowly, Hanna rose from his chair. He felt in his pockets for a handkerchief, but unable to locate one reached for his table napkin and dabbed his eyes.

"General Booth," he said in a slightly choked voice, "from the bottom of my heart I thank you. Before today you were just a name to us. If I might say so, a distant, almost eccentric figure, but now we know you. We know what you stand for. We know what makes the Salvation Army the unique, remarkable organization it is. General, for myself, and I suspect many more here today, you have my recognition. You have my support. May God bless you and the Salvation Army. If anyone else in this assembly wishes to express their thanks to General Booth they may do so now." Hanna sat down, and touched his eyes again with the napkin.

One by one noted figures of the Washington scene rose to speak. Vice-President Fairbanks, Speaker Henderson, Justice Brewer, Senators Cockrell and Hoar, and others stood to acknowledge the humble General of a Christian Army.

The following day the General went to the White House to meet President Roosevelt. The President asked about the Army's work among prostitutes and ex-prisoners. He also enquired about the farm colonies, some of which were now well established in the United States.

The meeting was informal and brief, as the President was called away on a matter of urgency. But Booth had been impressed by the relaxed atmosphere in which the President had conducted it.

Booth then returned to New York, where he bade farewell to Booth-Tucker and the other officers at American Headquarters, and boarded ship for home. In all he had visited fifty-two towns and cities, traveled nearly sixteen thousand miles and, it is estimated, addressed 300,000 people.

40

An Audience With the King

Queen Victoria had never smiled upon the Salvation Army. To her dying day she had no time for any army but her own. Her son, King Edward VII, was more sympathetic. He granted Booth an audience.

On the day in June 1904 that he was to visit His Majesty, Booth went first to inspect the preparations for the International Congress, which was to be held that week at the Strand Hall. After discussions with Bramwell, Lawley, and Colonel Kitching about the Congress, he prepared himself to meet the King of England by washing his hands in a workman's bucket.

He then went to Buckingham Palace by hansom cab. Booth faced this interview with more trepidation than that with President Roosevelt. He had loved the informality of the American leaders. He could not expect the same from the King of England, Emperor of India.

He was ushered into the impressive reception room where King Edward waited. Booth did not notice the beautiful panelled walls and the portraits of previous monarchs hung on them. His eyes were on the King, dressed informally in a dark suit, his neatly clipped and tapered white beard contrasting with his dark, bushy mustache.

"I am delighted to meet you, General Booth," said the King. They shook hands.

"You are doing a good work—a great work, General Booth. Do come and sit down," instructed the King.

"Thank you, Your Majesty," repeated Booth as he sat in the armchair he had been directed to. "I am grateful to Your Majesty for granting me this interview."

"Not at all—I am interested in such work as yours. Always have been. I have supported the work in the hospitals, as you no doubt know," said King Edward.

"Yes, Lord Carrington has told me some of Your Majesty's experiences in slumdom," Booth responded with a smile.

"Ah, yes, Lord Carrington is an old friend of mine. Tell me, General Booth, how did you begin your work?" asked the Sovereign.

Booth smiled again. He stroked the straggly strands of his beard as he reflected on the events of 1865. He felt more relaxed now. "It was after I left the Methodist Church, Your Majesty, and was working as an independent evangelist," began the General. Booth continued the story, occasionally interrupted by a question from King Edward.

When Booth concluded his tale, the King asked, "What are your hobbies, General? What do you do for recreation?"

Booth had not been asked that one before, so he paused for reflection, then answered, "Sir, some men have a passion for art, others have a passion for riches; I have a passion for souls."

The king smiled, and deciding to draw the audience to a close, stood. Booth did likewise. "General, this has been most stimulating, most stimulating," said the King enthusiastically.

"It has indeed, Your Majesty," agreed Booth. "I suppose I may tell my people that Your Majesty—"

King Edward broke in, "Tell them I have been delighted to meet their distinguished leader."

"And may I say that Your Majesty watches our work with interest?" questioned the General.

"Yes! Yes!" he replied emphatically.

"And regards its success as important to the well-being of the empire?" Booth asked daringly.

"Certainly! Certainly!" responded the King.

They shook hands in farewell. "May God bless Your Majesty. I shall pray for you," promised Booth.

The King bowed his head slightly and looked up again straight into Booth's eyes. "Thank you, General," he said with feeling.

Booth turned to leave. Faced with a choice of two doors, he hesitated for a moment, and then moved to go through the nearest one.

"No, General, try this one," directed the king, pointing to the other door. "Thank you for coming."

The embarrassed Booth said, "Oh, yes, Your Majesty—thank you," and left the room.

41

Booth's Final Travels

Shortly after the International Congress, Booth agreed to a plan that he should do a tour of Britain by motor vehicle. Booth was never one to despise the advantages of modern inventions. The car convoy, carrying Booth and his party, left London on August 9, traveling along the south coast as far as Land's End in the west. With him were two of his most faithful associates, Cadman and Lawley, and a reporter, Harold Begbie, eventually to be Booth's biographer. From Land's End they went north through England into Scotland, as far as Aberdeen, and then south along the east coast back to London.

Booth was seventy-five. At times the journey seemed too much for him, but he was so well received in cities, towns, and villages that he felt he must continue. For the whole of the tour he felt exhausted. Dyspepsia, a problem for most of his life, plagued him, and for the second half of the journey his throat was so sore that he found speaking in public difficult. It was also during this tour that he began to notice that his eyesight was failing. But his heart was cheered by the warmth of the public's response. Gone were the days when General William Booth was regarded as a good target for stones, mud, and rotten fruit. In just under a month, he traveled over twelve hundred miles and spoke at over one hundred meetings.

The following year Booth made a whirlwind tour of corps in New Zealand and Australia. His stopover in the Holy Land was a disappointment to him. Visiting sites of antiquity, however sacred, was little to his liking. Booth, even in his mid-seventies, remained a man of action. He gave a series of meetings while there to

172

smaller congregations than he was used to, mainly to tourists, and the response was minimal. Two Americans came forward after one sermon and were led to the Lord.

On his return home his health continued to worsen. His eyesight was still declining, his voice was weakening, a permanent feeling of weariness accompanied his waking hours, and insomnia had become a problem. But the General marched on!

Tales of the deeds of Bullard, Duce, and Yamamuro in Japan had moved his heart, and he determined to visit that mysterious land in the east.

His reception in Kyoto in May 1907 was beyond his wildest dreams. An enormous crowd gathered at the railway station to greet him. Various dignitaries, including members of the military, were on the welcoming committee. Booth addressed the throng through an interpreter before going to his host's home. Along the route were hundreds of people waving the Japanese flag and the Union Jack. He spoke that night in the city hall to a packed audience, the enthusiasm of which surprised him. At Kobe hundreds came forward at the invitation at the end of the two meetings held there.

The antipathy he had expected before his arrival in Japan did not materialize until his final meeting, which was held in a theater in Tokyo. The hall was packed, and at the rear was a group shouting down the General. "Kill him! Kill the General!" they called. "We won't kill his body. We will kill his soul!"

"We don't want your Jesus in Japan," came a voice from another part of the theater. Speakers, European and Japanese, were drowned out by the hecklers.

Order was not restored until the arrival of the police, who removed the ringleaders. This allowed the meeting to continue without further serious disruption. But officials, sensing the danger of the situation, insisted that a scheduled outdoor meeting for later that day be canceled.

Booth's determination continued to overcome his increasing physical limitations. He knew nothing about retirement. While souls were dying without Christ, how could he possibly retire?

He had longed to campaign in Rhodesia since his meeting with Cecil Rhodes after the publication of *In Darkest England*. Booth had followed his career with interest, if not always sympathy. Rhodes had died in 1902, but Booth still had that dream. Sadly, it was a dream to be left unfulfilled. He was always stopped by some difficulty or other from visiting that land. Even when he toured neighboring South Africa in 1908, word of persistent unrest in Rhodesia caused his advisors to insist that he content himself just with a visit to Africa's most southern nation.

The General was given an interview with Prime Minister Merriman shortly after his arrival in Cape Town. He then went to Johannesburg, Bloemfontein, Pietermaritzburg, and Durban. He was well received by the English and black people, but was largely ignored by the Boers.

The days of overseas trips were fast coming to an end. Short visits to Europe were still on his agenda, but, aged nearly eighty, travels farther afield were now beyond him.

42

Failing Sight

*I*n November 1908 William Booth went to his birthplace, Nottingham, to see Dr. Bell-Taylor about the cataracts on his eyes. Reading had become almost impossible. He could only see the largest of type, and though he could still write, it was very difficult. He returned to London and visited Guy's Hospital in early December, where the hospital's chief ophthalmologist, Mr. Charles Higgens, examined his eyes.

It was decided to do the operation to remove the cataracts in Booth's own home at Hadley Wood. A makeshift operating table was set up in an upstairs room.

As Booth entered the room, assisted by Colonel Lawley, he smiled at the surgeon, whose figure he could make out in the specially installed electric light. "You are ready for me, then, Mr. Higgens?" he asked.

"Yes, General," responded Higgens. "If you just sit down for a moment my assistant will anaesthetize your eyes."

Booth sat down, obediently submitted to the anaesthetist's ministrations, and waited. After the drug took effect, he was led to the operating table and helped up on it.

Higgens worked quickly. The lenses were removed, and the operation was over in a shorter time than it had taken to prepare for it. Booth's eyes were bandaged and he was put to bed.

A few days later Lawley burst into the General's room. "General, a telegram for you!" he said excitedly.

"Well, read it then. It's not something I can do for myself at the moment," said Booth. His tone was grumpy.

Lawley ignored the General's mild rebuke. "It's from the

Queen, General," he said. "It reads, 'Have felt so much for you, and hope the operation is successful, and trust you are getting on toward complete recovery, and that the sight you need so much will soon be completely restored. THE QUEEN.' "

A short silence followed before Booth spoke. "Read it again, Colonel."

Lawley complied.

"We must send a reply straightaway, Lawley," the General decided. "What shall we say? The question was addressed to himself. "How about, 'General Booth thanks Her Majesty for her gracious sympathy'?" Lawley had pulled a pencil from a pocket in his uniform, snatched a sheet of paper from the General's bedside table, and took the dictation sitting on the bed.

"Let me see!" Booth reflected for a moment. "Continue, '. . . with him in the operation he has found necessary, and for the gracious'—no, cross out 'gracious,' make it 'kind'—'expressions in her telegram.' " He paused again, then continued, " 'Mr. Higgens has just seen the eye and says that it could not possibly be doing better. The General begs to offer his best wishes for Her Majesty's happiness.' Read that back, Colonel."

Lawley read his notes.

"Send it immediately, Lawley. Don't keep Her Majesty waiting," instructed Booth.

"No, General, I won't. I will attend to it right away," said Lawley, rising from the bed and leaving the room.

The operation proved only moderately successful, but Booth continued to work from his home. He began his preparations for a big rally at the Congress Hall at the end of February, and a tour of the Continent after that.

On February 8 he received a letter from King Edward, with a check for one hundred guineas. The letter read: ". . . toward the great work in which you and your officers are, with such success, engaged."

After his short campaign in Europe Booth had a second operation in April. This proved no more successful than the first.

With determination, rather than physical strength, he embarked upon another motor tour of Britain, his sixth. While in Herefordshire, Booth suffered a worsening pain in the right eye. He decided to continue the tour in spite of the pain, and he and his party entered Wales, stopping at Newport. In Newport a doctor was summoned. He examined the eye, and insisted that the tour be canceled, so that Booth could return to London to visit Charles Higgens. Booth reluctantly agreed.

Higgens was shocked at the condition of the eye. It had deteriorated badly. He conducted a third operation in August.

The General lay in a deep sleep for over twenty-four hours after the operation, but eventually emerged from it, thrashing around in the bed. He uttered dazed cries of "Where am I? Where am I? What has happened?"

His nurse rushed to his bedside to try to calm him. "Everything's all right, General. You are in your own bed," she said. As his frenzy gradually subsided, she went to get Dr. Higgens.

Booth was in a semi-conscious state. He was unaware of the passing of time, unaware of everything except a dull ache in his eye and the smell of carbolic.

The doctor eventually entered his room, pulled up a chair and sat beside the old warrior. "General," he said slowly, "we have had to remove your eye. It was dangerous to leave it there any longer, I'm afraid."

Booth was still only partly awake, but he heard and understood the news. He had half-expected it anyway. The two men did not speak for a while. Booth could hear the distant sounds of traffic outside his home. "Yes, Mr. Higgens, thank you. I am grateful. I can still see with the other one," he said triumphantly. He tried to focus his remaining eye. "Well, a little at least," he said in more subdued tones.

Before the end of October, the eighty-year-old campaigner was preaching again at the Congress Hall. The following month he went to Horfield Prison, just outside Bristol. He traveled there with Railton and Lawley, and was met by local Salvation Army officers at the gates. While the Salvationists waited in the Governor's office, the convicts, men and women, were assembled in the courtyard. The women in white caps, with shawls over dull brown dresses, and the men in two-piece uniforms stood waiting quietly for the General.

Booth and his party entered the courtyard. The General was helped into an open motor vehicle, which he was to use as a platform. His voice was unsteady, his legs even more so, but he preached the Gospel message with his usual earnestness.

At the end, he told them that he would leave behind some of

his officers to counsel those who were concerned about their souls. Over thirty were counseled, and all but two of them came to the Lord.

The General was nearly blind and his body was frail, but his mind was still active. He saw the need for improving the Army's work in prisons. They had to gain more frequent access to the convicts. "How could this be done?" he asked himself. "Well, if I am now an acquaintance of kings and presidents, why should I be afraid to go to the top? I will see the man responsible for His Majesty's prisons." So Booth made an appointment to see Britain's Home Secretary.

Lawley accompanied him to Whitehall, and they were shown into the Home Secretary's office. He was a man of medium height and build, with a merry twinkle in his eye. "Welcome, General Booth," he said, extending his hand, and shaking the General's. "Do sit down."

Lawley guided him to a vacant chair. "It is very kind of you to see me, Mr. Churchill," said Booth, sitting down. "I believe that the matter we have to discuss is one of concern not just for the Salvation Army, but for the country as a whole."

"My time is yours, General. Tell me your plan," said Winston Churchill.

"You are, I know, familiar with the work of the Salvation Army. We have a unique organization, and we minister to sections of the community that are usually neglected by the established churches. My prime concern at the moment is the occupants of His Majesty's prisons," began Booth.

"As far back as 1883, an officer of ours began meeting convicts as they came out of prison in Australia, to try to place their feet on right pathways. So successful was his work that we have introduced this practice in many countries, including Britain. Our officers have also, on occasion, spoken with success at a number of prisons here. What I believe we need is greater access to the prisoners. If we can convert more of these men and women in the prisons, when they leave the confines of jail they will be useful members of society, instead of the bad influence they were before imprisonment."

Churchill did not appreciate a lecture. But this old man, by reputation and personality, had a quality that made one want to listen. "How would you propose to do this, General?" he asked.

"Well, I have a three-fold plan, Mr. Churchill. First, that my officers be allowed to hold a mission at least once a year in every prison in the country." Booth cleared his throat. "Secondly, to hold a religious musical meeting every quarter in each prison. We have many fine bands, as I am sure you know."

"You have indeed," commented Churchill.

"And thirdly, to hold a private meeting with any converts once a week," concluded the General.

At the end of the discussion Churchill excused himself, saying, "Just one moment, if we may, General Booth?" He leaned over and whispered to the two civil servants sitting with him. After what seemed forever, he turned his attention back to Booth. "General, we like your plan. We will consider it, and let you know accordingly."

"Thank you, Mr. Churchill. I thank you from the bottom of my heart," responded Booth. "When will we hear from you?"

"We will have to investigate the practicalities of your plan with the prison governors, of course. Let's say, a month at the most," promised the Home Secretary.

Churchill rose from his seat, and Lawley moved toward the General to help him up. As Booth got to his feet Churchill walked to his side and took his arm. He gently began to lead the old man to the door. "Tell me, General," he asked, "am I converted?"

The General hesitated, but though Churchill was an important politician, he could not compromise. "No, Mr. Churchill," he answered, "you are not converted, but I think you are convicted."

Churchill smiled. "You can see what is in me."

"What I am most concerned about is not what is in you at the present, but the possibilities in the future."

Churchill pouted. "Thank you for coming, General," he said. "It has been a most interesting discussion." He opened the door, and shook hands with Booth and Lawley.

"Thank you, again, Mr. Churchill. God bless you!" said Booth as he left the office. Lawley took his General by the arm, and led him out of the building into the waiting vehicle.

Further discussions were held between Bramwell and officials from the home office, and in March of the following year broad agreement to Booth's plan was announced.

43

Booth's Last Speech

*T*oward the end of January 1912 Booth had risen after a restless night. Leaving his upstairs room, he leaned heavily on the banisters as he negotiated the stairs. Suddenly he missed his footing and fell down the remainder of the flight. Bramwell, who was in the ground floor study going through some papers, heard the crash, rushed to the staircase and found the General sitting at the bottom, dazed.

"Are you all right, father?" Years of saying "General" seemed to end in a moment of concern.

Booth rubbed his head. "I think so, Bramwell. I don't think I have any broken bones. I banged my head, but you always said that was the hardest part of me."

His son laughed nervously, and helped the General to his feet. Bramwell led him to the living room and made him comfortable on the settee. "I will call the doctor," said Bramwell. The old General raised no objection.

Though there seemed no obvious repercussions from the fall, his strength continued to decline. His will to wage war, however, did not. A month later he went to Europe for the last time, speaking at meetings in Holland.

W. T. Stead paid a visit to Booth early in April. The General was in his study writing a letter to Eva in large, rather spidery letters, which he himself could barely see.

"Good morning, General," greeted the newspaper man. "I've just come to say 'cheerio.' I'm off to America next week." Stead knew the old man did not have much longer to live, and wanted to say goodbye without it appearing too final.

"America, eh!" exclaimed the General. "How I love America. Would you permit me a little righteous jealousy, Stead?"

The editor laughed. "Indeed, General! I am visiting some friends in the newspaper business in New York and Boston. I am looking forward to it very much. I'll be going on that new White Star liner that's just been completed."

"Oh, yeah! Bramwell was telling me about that one. What's its name?" asked Booth.

"The *Titanic*. It should be quite an experience. They say she is a magnificent ship. Well, General, I will say farewell," he said, extending his hand to the seated Salvationist. "God bless you!"

"God bless you, Stead," responded Booth. "Good bye!"

Ten days later W. T. Stead went to meet his Maker, four months before General William Booth, a victim of the most famous of all sea disasters.

Booth's final public appearance was in May, a month after his eighty-third birthday. It was held at a packed Albert Hall in London. When he stood to speak, Lawley took him by the arm and led him slowly to the rostrum. To the 10,000 people gathered he looked a mere shadow of the man who had had such a profound effect upon the lives of so many. But when he began to speak, he was shadow-like no longer. True, his voice did not have the clarity of earlier years. Occasionally he stumbled over words. But the dynamism was still there, the power. The crowd was hushed. No jeers, no cheers greeted the veteran campaigner's words, just tears.

"Very shortly," he began, "I am going into dry dock for repairs. At such a time I find myself reflecting upon my life's work. Why have I done it? Should I have chosen some other sphere of service? Should it have had a different emphasis?

"I might have chosen as my life's work the housing of the poor. But has not the Salvation Army done something in this direction? If you look abroad, you will find hundreds and thousands up and down the world who tonight have comfortable homes through the influence of the Army." The General seemed to sway a little, but held tightly to the lectern. Lawley half-stood, in case his General needed his support.

"I might have given myself up to the material benefit of the working classes. I might have drawn attention to the small rates of wages and striven to help them in that direction. But have we not done something for them? Are there not tens of thousands who, but for the Army, might have been almost starved?" The General was steadier now, and Lawley sat back in his seat.

"I might have given myself up to temperance reform, which is a most important business. But has not the Salvation Army done something in that direction? Every Salvationist the world over is a strict abstainer from intoxicating liquor, and the children are growing up to follow in their parents' footsteps. Tens of thousands of the most devilish and abandoned drunkards that the world has ever known have been reached and reclaimed.

"I might have chosen as my life's object the physical improvement and health of the people by launching out on a medical career. But we have done something in the way of medical aid, and possess at the present time twenty-four hospitals while others are coming into existence.

"I might have chosen to devote my life to the interests of the criminal world. But many prisoners have been admitted to our homes in this country during the year. We have done something for the criminal, but it is only the commencement of a mighty work the Army is destined to do for the unhappy class.

"I might have tried to improve society by devoting myself to politics. But I saw something better than belonging to any Party— that by being the friend of every Party I was far more likely to secure the blessing of the multitude, and the end I had in view.

"The object I chose all those years ago embraced every effort, contained in its heart the remedy for every form of misery and sin and wrong to be found upon the earth, and every method of reclamation needed by human nature. It is, of course, the Gospel of Jesus Christ.

"It is this Gospel that houses the poor, benefits the working class, promotes temperance and good health, reforms criminals, and transcends politics. It is Jesus Christ who changes lives and makes all these things possible. It is Christ only who is the answer to the problems and struggles." The old man looked and sounded weary, but his zeal and compassion had not lessened one bit.

"Is the Salvation War coming to a close? This war is just beginning. My part is coming to an end. But while I still have breath, I commit myself to strive for the Lord and those who need Him. While women weep as they do now, I'll fight; while little children go hungry as they do now, I'll fight; while men go to prison, in and out, in and out, I'll fight; while there yet remains one dark soul without the light of God, I'll fight. I'll fight to the very end! Fellow Salvationists, the war is not over. Win it for Jesus Christ!"

He stopped speaking, and half-turned to Lawley, who rose to aid him. They went through the back door and into a room at the rear, where the General collapsed in a chair, exhausted.

The audience remained silent, save for the sound of people crying. General William Booth of the Salvation Army had spoken in public for the last time.

44

Promoted to Glory

*I*n May Charles Higgens performed an operation on Booth's remaining eye. Again it was done at Booth's home. Higgens and his assistant were satisfied with their work, and quietly confident. There were encouraging signs immediately after the operation. But these were soon to vanish.

Booth's daughter, Lucy Booth-Hellberg, nursed him. A few days after the operation she noticed a discharge coming from the eye. Higgens was again summoned. He examined the eye, and told Lucy and Bramwell that it did not look hopeful.

"May we have a second opinion, Mr. Higgens?" asked Bramwell.

"You may, indeed," replied Higgens. "Churton Collins is the man. Try him."

Churton Collins came. He examined Booth's eye, and pronounced him blind—permanently blind.

Bramwell informed his father of the verdict. The General turned to his son unseeing, and said, "Bramwell, I have done what I could for God and for the people with my eyes. Now I shall do what I can without my eyes."

He continued his war from home—letters to his family and other officers, others to the *War Cry* and various politicians. He could not see, but he could still think and speak, and there was the admirable Lawley to put his words on paper. But his overall condition continued to deteriorate, and his memory was failing.

During the first week in August Bramwell visited his father. He found him in a distressed state, sitting in an armchair in his study.

"Chief, can you spare me a few moments?" he said, his voice charged with emotion.

"Yes, General, what is it?" asked Bramwell, sitting in the chair next to the old warrior.

"I want you to promise me that when my voice is silent, and I am gone from you, you will use such influence as you possess with the Army to do more for the homeless of the world. The homeless men, mind! I am not thinking of this country only, but of all the lands," Booth urged.

"Yes, General, I understand."

"The homeless women, too!" he added. "Ah, my boy, we don't know what it means to be without a home. The homeless children! Oh, the children! Bramwell, look after the homeless," he emphasized. "Promise me!"

"Yes, General, I promise." Bramwell was not humoring the old man. He meant it.

Booth hesitated for a moment, then said, "If you don't, I shall come back and haunt you!"

Bramwell laughed. "I believe you would, too. Was there any other matter, General?"

"Yes, Bramwell. I have been thinking very much during the last few nights about China. I greatly regret that the Lord has not permitted me to raise our flag among that wonderful people. I want you to promise me that as soon as possible you will get together a party of suitable officers and unfurl our flag in that land. You will need money, I know that. But you will get money if you get the right people."

"Yes, General, I promise."

"It's a bargain, is it?" smiled the General. "Then let's shake on it."

Father and son shook hands, and then poured out their hearts to God in prayer.

Within days Booth was confined to bed. He had no further prolonged conversation with anyone. A few days later, in hesitant speech, he muttered, "Bramwell, the promises . . . the promises . . . the promises . . . "

Bramwell prompted, ". . . of God."

"The promises of God . . . are sure . . . are sure." His scrawny hand waved in the air to emphasize the point. "If you only believe."

On August 18 he lost consciousness, and all the members of the family living in England were called to his bedside. Two days later he suffered several violent coughing fits, which occasionally brought him back into a state of half-consciousness. Lucy tenderly wiped his face after each bout of coughing. The other members of the family took turns to kneel at his bedside.

"Bramwell . . . Bramwell." The voice was soft, but the name unmistakable.

"Yes, father," responded Bramwell, clasping the dying man's hand.

"I'm leaving you a bonnie handful, Bramwell . . . a bonnie handful. But Railton will be with you," he said quietly. They were to be his last words.

At 9 P.M., with a storm raging outside, so reminiscent of the death of Catherine, Booth's breathing quickened and his pulse weakened.

Bramwell leaned over to kiss his father.

"Kiss him for Eva," reminded Lucy.

Bramwell kissed him again. He picked up a cable from Eva in America, and placed it in the General's still right hand. It read, "Kiss him for me."

At 10:13 that evening General William Booth, founder of the Salvation Army, gave up his spirit, and was "promoted to Glory."

The next day it was announced to the world that "The General has laid down his sword."

In his dying hours Booth had been less than prophetic. Eleven months later George Scott Railton was to catch a train in Germany, sit back in his seat, close his eyes and die. Bramwell would not have Railton for long.

45

God's Soldier

For three days Booth lay in state at the Congress Hall at Clapton, and over 100,000 men and women, boys and girls, inched past to catch a final glimpse of "God's Soldier."

The suggestion was made that Booth should be buried in Westminster Abbey, but the Dean, who saw no harm in the Abbey being the last resting place of Charles Darwin, objected. It seemed more appropriate, anyway, that he should be buried alongside his wife and the poor of London, in Abney Park Cemetery.

On August 28, nearly forty thousand people attended the funeral service at Olympia. At the back of the enormous gathering sat Queen Mary, unknown and unrecognized, attended by the Lord Chamberlain, Lord Shaftesbury. The funeral brought together the poorest of the poor and the richest of the rich.

The next day Booth's body, which had rested overnight at International Headquarters, was carried out by seven pallbearers, Salvationists of varying ranks, from Commissioner John Lawley to Private Sam Chumbley. As they emerged from the building they saw an enormous throng of people, filling the full length of Queen Victoria Street.

The coffin was placed upon a long hearse, drawn by two chestnut horses. The pallbearers stood by it motionlessly as they waited for the cortege to leave. When it did they walked slowly beside it past the silent crowd. Walking immediately behind the hearse were Bramwell and Florence Booth, followed by other members of the family. Then came an immense parade of thousands of Salvationists, with an enormous band, drawn from

187

many Salvation Army Corps throughout Britain.

The procession moved slowly through the densely packed streets of the city of London. Past the Mansion House it moved, where the Acting Lord Mayor, Sir John Knill, stood silently to attention. The crowd watched in stillness as the cortege moved slowly north. Men and women lined the streets from the city to Stoke Newington, as the Salvationists took their beloved General to his final earthly resting place, beside his dear Catherine.

William Booth, the pawnbroker's assistant, died a man honored by the world.

It was part of the Foundation Deed of the Salvation Army that each General must choose his successor. Booth's choice remained until his death in lawyer Alfred Ranger's safe.

Ranger went to International Headquarters with the envelope the day after the General died. The office was crowded with senior officers anxiously awaiting the announcement of the new General—the Bramwell Booths, Lucy Booth-Hellberg, George Railton, Elijah Cadman, Adelaide Cox, and John Lawley among them.

Ranger pulled the envelope from his pocket and passed it around, that everyone might see that it had not been tampered with. It was then returned to him and, being blind, he gave it to his assistant, William Frost. Frost opened the envelope, took out the solitary sheet of paper it contained and read its message out loud:

"The second General of the Salvation Army is William Bramwell Booth."